Experience God . . .
  His Love . . .
  His Blessings . . .
  His Power . . .

Experience God . . .
    His Love . . .
    His Blessings . . .
    His Power . . .

Bobbi Hodges

Order this book online at www.trafford.com
or email orders@trafford.com

Most Trafford titles are also available at major online book retailers.

Printed in the United States of America.

ISBN: 978-1-4669-0146-9 (sc)
ISBN: 978-1-4669-0258-9 (e)

Trafford rev. 10/26/2011

www.trafford.com

North America & International
toll-free: 1 888 232 4444 (USA & Canada)
phone: 250 383 6864 ♦ fax: 812 355 4082

Contents

God created man to have a personal relationship with Him, but; for many people they feel the need to "experience", in order to believe. It is my prayer, as you walk through the pages of this book, you will indeed experience the love and fullness of God, as He gently touches your heart and soul as He calls you unto Himself.

May God Bless your pathway back to Him,
BJ Hodges

"The Lord is good to those whose hope is in Him, to the one who seeks Him"

Lamentations 2:25

Preface

Experience God . . . His Love . . . His Blessings . . . His power . . . is a book, specifically written with pre-Christians and new believers in mind. It's a tool or guide to bring clarity, and to separate the many biblical truths from myths and facts from fiction. This book sheds light on God's promises for your life, and helps to bring about protection from ignorance and rebellion, which will prevent you from experiencing God's exciting blessings and fullness of His promises. It also shares the truth of what many of today's Pastors fear to teach from the pulpit.

Experience God . . . His Love . . . His Blessings . . . His Power . . . brings encouragement, hope, and direction for a broken world facing the **end times.** It not only brings insight of God's awesome and prosperous plan for your life, but you will also be able to recognize the power, the faith, and the beauty that God has placed in you through His Son, our Lord, Jesus Christ.

God has purposed each of us with many assignments, and **Experience God . . .** is an assignment and instrument to help others come to know the Creator of all life, the Most High God, and the Knowledge and acceptance of Jesus Christ, our pathway home!

All profits from this assignment will be donated to *Wings of Eagles—International Fellowship of Christians and Jews,* under the direction of Rabbi Yechiel Eckstein. Thus keeping in covenant with our God. *Scripture:* **Genesis 12:3 "I will bless those who bless you (Israel) and whoever curses you (Israel) I will curse."**

ACKNOWLEDGEMENTS

A special thanks to a very dear friend, Kathy Graven. I am grateful and blessed for her expertise and knowledge of editing and the many hours she invested. A heartwarming thanks to my precious prayer partner, Tami Hoff, for all her prayers and encouragement. I am also, very blessed to have the love and support of my children, Linda Juliano, Stephen Hodges, Jeff Johnson and dear friend, Carol Gilbert.

Introduction

EXPERIENCE GOD . . . His Love . . . His Blessings . . . His power,

This is a book that allows you to Explore the characteristics of God Almighty, and learn to distinguish His voice and promptings from that of the voice of the enemy and the many influences of the world. Learn the ways God communicates with you on a personal level and know that His love is unconditional and faithful. Unlike His love, most of God's promises are conditional, and He freely blesses whom He chooses. Know what promises have what conditions attached.

Experience God's peace as He draws you into Himself and demonstrates His love for you. God created you for Himself, and His desire is to bless and prosper your life. Who else could possibly love you and understand your ways better than the very God who created you as His master piece.

Learn of the promises God has deliberately designed for your life, so you don't need to allow ignorance or rebellion to interfere and keep you from experiencing His blessings and the fullness of His promises. As you develop a personal relationship with your creator, the God Most High, you will have a clear understanding of how your prayers will move the hand and heart of God Jehovah, in order for you to receive His many blessings and favor.

Learn how to obtain financial freedom and break the chains of addictions. It's never too late for God to change your life for the better and to show you real security and love. Allow God to give you the life that is beyond your imagination. As He says in **Jeremiah 32:27 "I am the Lord, the God of all mankind. Is anything too hard for me?"** The old saying goes, if you want something you've never had, you need to do something you've never done. The first and most important ingredient, to have a richly blessed and exciting Christian life, is to have the Most High God with all His power, pilot your life.

We are living in the most exciting time in the history of the world. For we are the chosen generation to witness God bring forth the final days of His plans and promises for mankind. It's because of God's faithfulness, that believers and followers of Jesus Christ and servants of the only true God, is why they are not afraid of physical death, nor do they fear the **end times,** but instead, rejoice as we watch, with our very own eyes, prophecies come to pass. God is your strength, faith is your victory, and obedience is your compass. Learn to have faith <u>only</u> in God, not yourself, not other people, and not other things. The Bible says in Jeremiah 17:9 **"The heart is deceitful above all things and beyond cure. Who can understand it?"**

Why are many pastors and spiritual leaders afraid to tell *<u>all</u>* of God's truth, from the pulpit? How do you know who is a Christian and who is the hypocrite? Why do Christians say "born again" or are you saved and what does that all mean? Christians often appear to be confused or double minded, are they? There are so many different Christian churches that seem to believe so differently from one another, how can that be? What's the difference from religious and spiritual? If we are to follow the Bible, why does it seem so complicated? These are just a few of the often asked questions. **<u>Experience God . . . His Love . . . His Blessings . . . His Power,</u>** allows the Holy Bible to speak for itself and give you God's answers.

FORWARD

All profits from ***EXPERIENCE GOD . . . His Love . . . His Blessings . . . His Power,*** will be donated to Wings of Eagles (International Fellowship of Christians and Jews). This organization rescues the remnants of Israel from distressed countries, paying for their passage to Israel, as well as supplying food, shelter, and medical attention to the destitute.

God of Abraham, Isaac and Jacob (Israel), made an everlasting covenant with Abraham and his descendants, which God honors to this day;

Genesis 12:2 "I will make you into a great nation and I will bless you, I will make your name great, and you will be a blessing, I will bless those who bless you, and whoever curses you I will curse; and all people on earth will be blessed through you."

CHAPTER ONE

John 3:21 "But those who do what is right come to the light so others can see that they are doing what God wants."

WHAT GOD WANTS YOU TO KNOW

Obviously, there are many, many things our God Jehovah wants us to know, and the Holy Bible addresses all of them. However, **Experience God—His Love . . . His Blessings . . . His Power,** is a starter book, you can grow and build upon. Liken it to a starter home, a place that is essential for your healthy physical needs. This book provides information from the Holy Bible that is crucial for your spiritual needs. A home provides protection for your physical body against the elements of the weather, and the Holy Bible, information, provides protection for your spirit, from the evil elements of the world. When our spirit comes separated from it's creator, our God Jehovah, it will become diseased and die and then the body will also parish.

God has a specific purpose for each one of us to accomplish while on this earth, and each of us has a limited amount of time to complete our assignment. God gave us talent, ability, knowledge, desire, and the skill for each assignment. In how to live our lives, God gave us written instructions and answers to questions we might have, along with a map showing us the way back to Him and our forever home!

God wants us to know exactly what His Truth is and **_not the_** truth of the world, which are Satan's lies. Too many Christian church's, of today, are doing their congregation, the world, and themselves a dangerous disservice by watering down the Word of God. They are delivering half truths and withholding consequences from disobediences. It appears they do this for, perhaps, better ratings, bigger congregations, and more money; all the time giving people a false sense of security. It's like telling a child it's not a good idea to play with matches, without telling the child matches cause fire and fire can burn or even kill you. Many church going folks are living in sin and not even aware of it, and many are hypocrites and seem to not know or not believe there will be a consequence to pay for this behavior. Is it any wonder much of the world looks at the Christian church with skepticism, confusion, contempt and some with hatred? I, truly, do not know the reasons why some churches choose not to teach all of God's truth, but I do understand many folks only want to hear about the good promises and blessings, from God, and not want to hear about His wrath or consequences, if we disobey, but withholding the truth is the same as lying.

All Pastors, Bishops, Ministers, Priests, teachers or anyone else behind the pulpit, needs to step up and teach the Word of God the way it is Written. They have a responsibility to teach God's Word in its entirety and leave the results up to God, and if folks are offended by God's message, He will take care of that as well. **James 3:1 "Dear brothers and sisters, not many of you should become teachers in the church, for we who teach will be judged more strictly".**

If ever people needed to hear the whole Truth of God's Word, it is now! We are living in the end times, and everything is right on God's time schedule. Satan has a firm foothold in the world and his evil will increase with each passing day. Wrong becomes right, and good becomes bad, mocking Christians and world economic disasters, will increase and so will natural disasters, and personal catastrophes; but, none of these things are a surprise to God. Nonetheless, these are warnings signs for His people, that the end of time is approaching. As Satan's evils are apparent, the Holy Spirit's Power will also become more prevalent. God knows the end of this story and He wants you to know it too.

God wants you to know that He loves you so much that it is impossible for the human mind to understand or comprehend the scope of His love for you. With His soft voice, He will constantly call you back to Him because more than anything He wants you back with Him for eternity. He loves you so much He came to earth as man to pay your sin debt, on the cross, and to show you the pathway home. God's Love, for you, cannot be trumped!

God made you in His image; He gave you a loving heart and created your world with beauty, food and water. He has a storehouse of blessings, waiting for you to accept them. His favor and blessings will ease your way through life's journey and He will make the crooked path straight. His heart breaks when you reject Him and He feels the hurt when you refuse His ways, for it is His ways that will protect and bring you back to Him.

God knows absolutely everything about you and He wants you to know Him. He wants you to have a personal relationship with Him, and He wants you to rely on Him for your every need and desire. He is your provider, your wisdom, your happiness, and your shield, for He is your God. **Deuteronomy 6:5** **"And you must love the Lord your God with all your heart, all your soul, and all your strength."** Remember, love is a choice.

God wants you to know that you need to choose your words and actions wisely, for you have much power in the tongue. With your tongue you can choose to bless or curse, express love or hate, accept or rebuke, tell truth or lies; either way, your words will come back on you. So, is it not better to be blessed than cursed, to be accepted instead of rejected, to be given the truth opposed to lies, to be loved rather than hated? Use your power (tongue) to bless, edify, love, and to praise and worship God, our Heavenly Father. Pray God's Word and find victory, for God's Word will never return void. This means pray God's Word (Scriptures) back to Him. He didn't forget what He said in His word, but it shows you, your heart. So trust Him for what He promised.

God wants you to know there are two driving forces on earth. First is God Jehovah, the creator and savior of mankind. The God of heaven and earth, the God who will teach you His ways and save you from the evil one. **Luke 19:10** **Son of Man came to seek and to save those who are lost".** The other force is God's enemy and ours, Satan, who was kicked out of heaven. **Luke 10:18** **The Lord said "I saw Satan fall like lightning from heaven."** The father of evil, the devil **John 8:44** **He was a murderer from the beginning. He has always hated the truth, because there is no truth in him. When he lies, it is consistent with his character; for he is a liar and the father of lies. "1Peter 5:8** **Your enemy the devil prowls around like a roaring lion looking for someone to devour."** Satan hates humans and he will destroy as many as possible for he, also, knows the end is near and he is running out of time. The devil will trick and deceive and lead you to destruction and straight to hell if you give him the opportunity.

There is a Heaven, **Genesis 14:19 God Most High creator of heaven and earth."** and there is a hell, **Matthew 5:22 will be in danger of the fire of hell".** God has prepared a place in heaven for you, and He has prepared a place called hell for Satan and his demons. He did not intend for humans to go to hell, however, when Satan brought sin to earth, and many chose to follow him, therefore, Satan will lead them into hell if they don't turn back and ask God to forgive their sins. Mankind only has two choices, God or Satan, Heaven or Hell, and to say there is no heaven or hell, or there is no God or devil, is a lie directly from Satan whom you are following if you believe there is no God or there is no devil.

In the scope of eternity, life is but a few days on earth. We all have the same destiny; death, and life as we know it on earth will end, and God will bring judgment on all. **Ecclesiastes 9:2 No man knows when his hour will come".**

God wants you to know, because man is made in His image, our life is also eternal, and where you spend it depends on your choice. He loves us so much that He gave us a free will to use in making our choice. God loves everyone and is ready to forgive those who turn to Him. We are all sinners and we all need His forgiveness. It is the blood of Jesus Christ that washes our sins away and it is His righteousness that makes us acceptable for heaven. Sin can't be in heaven or in the presence of God, that's why we have a savior. For those who do not turn to Christ to be made clean, they will automatically choose Satan, and their eternal home will be hell. God will love and miss those who choose not to be with Him, and how, very, heartbreaking it would be if the last thing you heard God say:

My son/daughter (your name), I will love you always
And miss your precious smile and all the good in you.
I loved you before you were formed in your mother's
Womb. I loved you so much I sacrificed my only Son to
Suffer for you, so you could have a pathway back to your
Eternal home, heaven. I am so sorry you refused my offer.
Now the door is closed and it's too late, as judgment
has been passed.

Dear friends, take this time to reflect on your life and know, right now, today, it's not too late to make the right forever choice. Don't let this life on earth be the best thing that will ever happen to you; God has, not only a wonderful, rich full life for you, but, also a fantastic future planned, just for you!

Repetition is a great teacher, for us humans; and because of the enormous importance, of many topics, that pertains to our lives now and after-life, you will notice that many statements our reiterated, throughout this book.

CHAPTER TWO

Deuteronomy 7:9 "Understand, that the Lord your God is indeed God. He is the faithful God who keeps His covenant, and lavishes His unfailing love on those who love Him and Obey".

EXPERIENCE GOD AND WHO HE IS

When I was a young child I believed God sat in Heaven and kept track of all my wrong doings, which seemed to be many. I didn't know anything about having a relationship with God, nor would I even know what that was supposed to look like. I didn't really expect anything from God because I knew I couldn't be good enough to receive anything, so why ask, was my thought. My knowledge of right and wrong was what I was taught from my parents and teachers. Thank goodness we didn't have television as a learning tool, as we do today. Imagine how confusing it could be for a child of today, having conflicting messages coming from so many different avenues. Hind sight being 20/20, I can tell you with certainty that without the Father, Son, and Holy Spirit at the forefront of your life, you will never know truth, and you will never experience all the good God has planned for your life.

As Christians we all have the responsibility to share with others God's truth, and who He is, how much He loves you and me, and how much He wants to have a meaningful relationship with us. On the other hand, it is God alone who draws and calls you to come back to Him. He can and will change you to be the person He has purposed and designed you to be. **Philippians 2:13 Not in your own strength for it is God who is all the while effectually at work in you energizing and creating in you the power and desire, both to will and to work for His good pleasure and satisfaction**

and delight. (Amplified) You and I were given the responsibility and opportunity to choose who we are going to follow and trust, serve, believe and love. **"Blessed is the man who makes the Lord his trust" Psalms 40:4 NIV**

God is calling you now, to come to Him, and for this reason you are reading this book. For only God knows who has a hardened heart against Him and who is ready to know Him and obey His calling. God will always choose the method that works best in getting your attention and to open your eyes, your ears, and your heart to be receptive to His promptings. God has the desire to fellowship and communicate with you as an individual. His very own nature is to love you and extend His Grace and Blessings. His heart is to bless you with His best. We can either choose to love God and follow Him or one can choose to follow Satan and be the enemy of God. There are no other choices. That's why we are here so that we can make our choice. That is our *free will,* given to us by God.

Jesus was sent to earth to do the *Will* of God and to redeem man from sin. God gave us a *free will* so we could choose who we are going to serve and obey. Because God loves and values us so much, He sent His only Son, Jesus Christ, to reclaim us and show us the way back to Him. He wants us to choose Him and do His *Will.* Perhaps now is the time to get acquainted and develop your relationship with our God, Lord. **Jesus said, "No one can come to Me unless the Father who sent Me draws him" "It is written in the prophets, "AND THEY SHALL ALL BE TAUGHT OF GOD,' Everyone who has heard and learned from the Father, comes to me." John 6:44, 45**

Allow yourself to feel the excitement deep within your soul, knowing that God is actually calling you, personally. God is giving you the opportunity to know Him as our Almighty God Jehovah, the Father God of Abraham, Isaac and Jacob, the God of Heaven and earth, the God of you and me. This is the God of the Holy Bible; this is our creator, our Heavenly Father! There are many gods but only one creator and true God, and this God adores you and me. **Ephesians 2:10 "For we are God's masterpiece."**

God knows, absolutely, everything about us, from before our very first breath on earth to our hereafter. Nothing can be hidden from Him. God is so concerned about everything that goes on in our lives, that He finds nothing too trivial for us to pray about, He even numbered the hairs on our head! Do you know how many hairs are on your child's head? **Matthew 10:30 "and the very hairs**

of your head are numbered." Since He knows us so intimately, does it not make sense He wants us to know Him as well? God tells us to have no other gods, and we are to love and obey only Him. This is definitely, an invitation for us to establish a true and meaningful relationship with our creator; to know who He really is on a one on one level. Don't fall into the trap of so many others, that try life on their own terms, and when they fall short of their own expectations, or worse, their life becomes a disaster and they are left with sadness and despair and then ask the unanswered question, WHY . . . . and why is there not a better life for me? The disappointments, the hurts, and losses are too much to endure and they need something to change. Don't wait for failure or disaster, now is the time for that change.

It's not so much the unwillingness people have to know God, as it is their fear of knowing Him. Let's face it, if one does not know God's unconditional love and His forgiving heart, the idea of meeting or acknowledging our Holy God could be very intimidating and frightening; so much so, some people won't even talk about or even admit there is a Holy God.

We have all done wrong and experienced the emotion of unworthiness, but when this emotion is compounded with pride we have a recipe for a runaway. Pride will keep runaways from going home, even when they discover, life is too difficult to handle alone. Fear of change, fear of failure, fear of accountability before God, and the fear of the unknown will bring on anxiety and depression; all of which the enemy (Satan) plants and uses to keep us away from knowing our God. The believers, in our Lord, know of His love and forgiveness and will repent. But for the nonbeliever, this all becomes too overwhelming and they try to find comfort and safety in denying God's existence. Many may feel their sins are just too great to be forgiven, and yet others may have unresolved issues and believe God is to blame for all their pain and disappointments. These are just a few reasons people give in rejecting God; ironically, these are some of the same reasons people have in coming to God. Just because one says he/she does not believe in God or Jesus Christ, does not make it true that God does not exist, and it will not lessen the accountability of their sins. Sin is sin regardless of what we might want to think or believe and there will be a day of reckoning.

When bad things happen beyond ones control and a supernatural intervention, known as a miracle is needed, who does the unbeliever cry out to, who is their god that can help? How much pain will they allow in their life, or how many awful situations and hardships will they endure before they give Our true God, our Creator an opportunity to bring them His help and peace? What will it take before you reach for God's hand?

God will allow circumstances in our lives, good or bad, whatever it takes for us to come back to Him. He is a jealous God and we are His creations and He wants us back with Him. Before we were born we were with God and He wants all of us back with Him, after this life. Regardless of the choice you make to return to Him or not, He will always love you. But only if you choose Jesus Christ's path, will you be allowed to return to your Heavenly Father. I know, many do not believe this, and they choose to follow their god of self, or worship their god of money, drugs, sex, environment, power or some other man made creation; but look around at the world today and see how these other gods are bringing pain, hopelessness, destruction and even physical and spiritual death upon man. God never intended for us to live this life without Him being the center of our lives. So for those who choose Jesus Christ, they can tap into His supernatural powers and have the life and blessings that God has designed for them, and all of His promises, through Jesus Christ.

God created us for His glory, fellowship, and purpose; He has a wonderful plan (**John 3:27** **"God in heaven appoints each mans work"**, for each our lives. He wants to be our friend, imagine that, just as He considered Abraham to be His friend. So, is it not reasonable to believe that God made a way for us to communicate and interact with Him, and is this not the ultimate privilege ever?

The most, unimaginable beautiful life possible, is available to all of us through Jesus Christ. Our lives should and could be the most purposeful and exciting journey ever. Our own way is so very different from what the Lord has planned for us. **Isaiah 55:9**
"As the heavens are higher than the earth, so are my ways higher than your ways and my thoughts than your thoughts."

You, too, can be plugged into the only source in all the world that has all the true answers you need to life's questions and also has the capacity and willingness to lead us down the right path for our happiness and success and to be complete in His *Will* and plan for our lives.

Only this Holy God of the universe, heaven and earth knows what the future holds and all knowledge and wisdom. God used the prophet Isaiah to tell of the coming and crucifixion of Jesus Christ, some 600 years before it happened, so, He would certainly know our future. The good news is, He is willing to reveal many things to you just because He loves you and wants you to have a bright future; after all, you are His creation of love. God is on your side, and all of us will have the opportunity to decide who's side we are on. Actually, God is everything you will ever need in this life. He is our strength and provider, **Philippians 4:19** **"and it is He who will supply all your needs from His riches in glory, because of what Christ Jesus has done for us."** He gives us wisdom and protection. He gives us the kind of love, far above anything, that mankind can offer. There are no words to describe the feeling of being engulfed in God's love, it's a Holy experience and this alone, is worth our investing ourselves to this one and only true God!

James 1:5 **"If any of you lacks wisdom, let him ask of God, who gives to all generously and without reproach, and it will be given to him." Proverbs 2:6 "For the Lord gives wisdom; from His mouth come knowledge and understanding."**

I know, to our human mind, it seems unlikely that our Holy God actually has a desire to fellowship and communicate with us as individuals; but the bible tells us it is God's heart and nature to love and bless us over and over and no one can stop His blessings on us, except our unbelief. Too often we allow our independence, stubbornness, and lack of faith to get in the way of God's *Will*. This interference can harden our hearts, and along with the unbelievers, this will keep us from hearing God when He speaks to us, and we will not recognize or understand the signs He puts in front of us, causing us to miss His instructions and blessings.

God doesn't expect us to be perfect, but He does expect us to be obedient and righteous, just as we expect our own children to obey.

God knows it is not possible for us to be sinless when we live in a sinful world, and that's why we need Jesus. Paul tells us in the book of Romans **"No matter which way I turn I can't make myself do right. I want to but I can't. When I want to do good, I don't and when I try not to do wrong, I do it anyway. Now if I am doing what I don't want to, it is plain where the trouble is: sin still has me in its evil grasp." Romans 7:18-20** God took care of our weakness by sending His precious Son, Jesus Christ, to be the blood sacrifice required for our sin. God cannot look upon sin, therefore, Jesus stands between us and God, acting as the filter so God can see us as righteous. It is this selfless sacrifice our Lord made, that makes it possible for us to have a personal relationship with our God Jehovah; through the power of Jesus Christ, we can obey our Lord. Jesus did not come to earth to condemn us, but to save us from the clutches of Satan. **Luke 19:10 "For the Son of man is come to seek and to save that which was lost."**

I think its difficult for us to comprehend this kind of unconditional love God demonstrated by sacrificing His only Son for payment of our sins. It is God's deep love for us that makes us special to Him. God claims us as His very own children, so shouldn't we claim Him as our heavenly Father? After all, He is the foundation of our life, and, only He can bless us with a fulfilled and prosperous life.

The first step for developing a personal relationship with God is to believe He is God and He has invited us to into a relationship with Him, for He alone, is God. Then we can go on our journey to find out what God is like and become sensitive to His voice and ways. Getting to know God is achieved, pretty much the same way it is when we meet new people in our lives; we spend quality time with them. The more time we spend together the more intimate we become, and so it is with God. You see, God is real. He is not a myth nor is He a fairy tale. He thinks, He feels, He hurts, He acts, He Loves, and He plans and we are His plan. **"I will come and do for you all the good things I have promised. I know the plans I have for you, says the Lord. They are plans for good and not for evil, to give you a future and a hope." Jeremiah 29:10; "and if you leave God's paths and go astray, you will hear a Voice behind you say, "No, this is the way; walk here." Isaiah 30:21**

Aren't you just a little bit curious what those plans and promises are, for your life? God can only do good things for us, as He is not capable of doing evil; in fact he hates evil. He actually causes things to work for our good. **Romans 8:28 "And we know that God causes everything to work together for the good of those who love God and are called according to His purpose for them."**

When we pray to God, we just need to speak from the depth of our heart and soul. We can tell Him anything, including what we truly believe, feel and think. God can handle it, and its okay to ask Him to reveal Himself to you. Talk with God the way you would talk with your best friend. Don't worry about how you should say something, it doesn't matter, just be yourself. God knows what you're saying, He reads your heart not your lips.

The Bible is the most valuable book you will ever possess. It's full of rich treasures and promises; it gives hope, where there is no hope, it gives direction to the lost, it teaches us how to be in favor with God. It will bring you joy and peace, for the Bible was written for you and me. The Bible is the inspired Word of God. He chose and inspired the writers in what to say and write, so every word written is of God. Read the Bible daily, because you don't want to miss out on what God is telling you, for this day and what it holds for you. You will discover it is loaded with His instruction, just for you, and you will be amazed to see how often He tells you how much He loves you. You will learn of God's plans and promises for you. The Bible tells us the promises are for those who love Him, and God will keep every promise He makes to you and me, for He is faithful, even if we are not. **Romans 3:4** speaks of God's faithfulness. All we need to do is ask. **James 4:2 "you do not have, because you do not ask God"** God will show you His character, His nature, and the way to His heart. Just let Him know that you want to know His truth, and, as only He can, He will reveal it to you. Let Him know you need His help to believe and worship. **Jesus said, "I will only reveal myself to those who love me and obey me. The Father will love them too, and we will come to them and live with them. Anyone who doesn't obey me doesn't love me." John 14:23,24**

It has been said, we will never experience true love until we first know the love of God; as we learn to love in the way that He teaches us to love, you too, will discover that His love, shows the way to true love. When we love and appreciate God completely, we will have the capacity to love others in the way God has intended. When we truly seek our Lord, He changes our hearts and reveals to us His sweetness, faithfulness, patience, forgiveness, sense of humor, and yes He does have a great sense of humor. He will show you His tenderness, protection and His glorious unconditional love!

Did you know to love someone is a choice? If this were not true Jesus would not have said, **"This is my command love each other" John 15:17** Love is a decision we make not an emotion we feel, although the two often blend together. It is easy to confuse love with emotions of infatuation or desires, but God will help us to identify our thoughts and feelings. Love is the fullness of God and when we show love to others we show the character of God. We choose to love God. We choose to love our parents, spouses, children, friends and self. We can choose to love all people, but that doesn't mean we need to love the wrongdoing or sinful ways of this world. Love the sinner and hate the sin.

As our relationship with the Lord develops, we become aware of God giving us new thoughts and ideas. This is one of God's way of giving us a glimpse or a view of His *will* and direction for our life. As each day passes He will reveal more and more of His plan that He has for us. God teaches through His Word (the Bible) so God will NEVER give us a thought or an idea that goes against His Word. This is another reason we need to be reading His Word daily. I once read an article that Billy Graham said, "when you pray, you are talking to God and when you read the Bible, God is talking to you." God will give you all the time you need or want with Him. He won't restrict your time with Him.

We can't respond to God's promptings if we don't know what He is telling us, and we won't know what He is saying if we don't read the Bible. Therefore, it would only make sense that we spend time in His Word (the Bible) so we can know Him better. You see, any of us can get information about God's character, likes, dislikes, etc., but that's all informational not relational. All relationships require personal commitment. It's no different with God; we need to invest our time, love, and our whole self. A relationship with God is dependent on our surrendering our entire being to Him. This means every part of our body, mind, soul, and every problem, every thought, our job, our money, obligations, everything, we give it all to God for then our life will be His, to do as He pleases. How do you surrender your life to God? Just tell Him your life is His and you only want to do His *will* and His plan. Surrender yourself daily!

Many people know of God, and many know God, but few people have a true relationship with Him. It's this relationship that gives us a look at the blueprint of what He has for our lives. Don't settle for anything less than having a full on relationship with God, for this is our God given right; a right given to us by God. This is where all the good stuff happens! His plan and promises come together. This is when our dysfunctional becomes functional, our empty becomes filled, our dark becomes light, and our sad becomes joy. We replace anger and bitterness with love. The greatest gift, is to know His heart and to feel and experience His love and presence!

God created each of us with a deep desire to know and love Him by placing a void in our hearts, that only He can fill, when we accept Him as our Lord and Savior. When people say; there must be more to life than this, or, everything will be fine once I make more money, everything will be fine when I get married, everything will be fine when I get divorced, everything will be fine when I get a new job, everything will be fine when I have a baby, everything will be fine when I get a drink, (alcohol), everything will be fine when I get a fix (drugs), everything will be fine when I get . . . , and the **everything list** goes on and on searching for something or someone to fill the void that is buried deep within us; turn to God, He is the filling for your void, He is the missing part for your life and He is the component that makes life work.

Most of our troubles we bring upon ourselves by being out of the will of God. That is not to say those who have a relationship with God never have trouble or disappointments, that's just not true. As long as we live in this world of sin and freewill, we will always have trials and tribulations and disappointments. The difference is when we obey and follow God's *will*, we bring less of the bad upon ourselves. God gave us all a freewill and He will not interfere with our freewill. Nonetheless, others freewill can and do become obstacles in our path. So, remember what others meant for evil, against us, God can change it for our good. Often people go through their hardships with a heavy and worried heart, but with the Lord we can go through the troubles with hope and confidence, knowing God is in control and all will workout for our good. God will never forsake or leave us, regardless how big the storms are, for He will walk us through the fire. Sometimes, God allows unfavorable circumstances in our lives to teach us, correct us or bring about His *Will* for us. Jesus tells us not to worry but trust in Him for every solution. **"Don't worry about tomorrow, for God will take care of your tomorrow"** Matthew 6:34 God will never abandon nor break His promises to us. He is trustworthy and compassionate toward us. **"For the Lord is faithful to His promises." "Blessed are all those who wait for Him to help them."** Isaiah 29:18 **"No, I will not abandon you or leave you as orphans in the storm . . . I will come to you"** John 14:18. God is faithful to us and He cares about every single thing that goes on in our lives, regardless, how insignificant we my believe it to be. Nothing is too trivial for God, and because of His unwavering love and faithfulness, we have security in Him. No insurance policy in the world can give us the security that our heavenly Father gives us. It's all about trust, and nothing is too big or too small for our God to handle. **"I am the Lord, the God of all mankind; is there anything too hard for me?"** Jeremiah 31:27

It's your faith, trust and love for God, that develops a relationship. Remember, love is a choice, and faith comes by hearing the Word of God. When we get into the relationship phase is when things really start to happen for us, because God now has our attention and commitment. You know God does not leave anything to chance. He plans everything for us and you can't shock or surprise Him. He has already seen this parade from beginning to end. He knows every crises and celebration we've had or will have. He knows every smile we've ever flashed and He knows every single tear we've shed, and nothing will ever happen without His knowledge; nothing can be hidden, and what's been done in the dark He will bring it to the light; in other words He knows absolutely everything that comes or will come into our lives, and only He can change or fix what is broken. He sees all the good and all the bad. He knows who will do us wrong and the wrong we will do. Because of our *free will*, God has given each of us, He will not intercede on our behalf or interfere unless we ask Him to do so. Hence the importance of daily surrender to Him.

To know God, is to love and trust Him as He takes you through this journey of life, and with Him, there are no regrets. He has a whole new world for you and He is just waiting for you to take His hand. He will take you places that one could only dream about. You will meet some of the most awesome people ever and you will not only have new dreams beyond your imagination, but you will see them come to pass. When challenging times come, and they will come, He will bring you through unscathed, unhurt and you will be wiser and stronger then you were. **Isaiah 43:2 When you go through deep waters and great trouble, I will be with you. When you go through rivers of difficulty, you will not drown.**

I will make the rough places smooth 42:16 God will equip you with everything you need; emotionally intellectually, physically, spiritually and materially to complete your journey here on earth.

God wants you to go through this journey of life being everything He designed you to be. You are so special to Him and He wants all good things for you. Just as your own children are to you, you would want only the best for them. The difference is we can't always give our children the best or do great things for them, but God can do great and wonderful things for His children, that are supernatural things. Things like changing a bad person to good, taking a damaged person and making him/her whole, He changes hearts, attitudes, minds and futures. He can remove sadness with joy, He removes despair with hope all because He loves you.

Here is a short interesting list of what happens when you choose to follow, obey and love God, yes, it is great to know your creator:

1 *God will give you spiritual ears to hear His voice.* **Job 37:5 God's voice thunders in marvelous ways; He does great things beyond our understanding NIV John 10:27 Jesus said "*My sheep listen to my voice*; I know them, and they follow me." NIV**

2. *Receive power and authority in the name of Jesus Christ.* **Ephesians 3:20 Now to Him who is able to do immeasurably more than all we ask or imagine, according to *His power that is at work within us.* NIV Colossians 2:10 and you have been given fullness in Christ, who is the head over every power and authority NIV Mark 16:17 those who believe shall *use my authority* TLB**

3. *Receive God's many blessings.* **Isaiah 56:3 And my blessings are for Gentiles, too, when they accept the Lord. TLB.**

4. *No need to worry; rest in God's peace.* **Matthew 6:25 Jesus said ". . . I tell you not to worry about everyday life, whether you have enough food and drink or enough clothes to wear. Isaiah 26:24 I will answer them before they even call to me. While they are still talking to me about their needs, I will go ahead and answer their prayers! Isaiah 26:3 He will keep in perfect peace all those who trust in Him TLB**

5. *Gods protection upon you.* **Isaiah 7:9 . . . if you want me to protect you, you must learn to believe what I say. John 10:28 I give them eternal life, and they will never perish. No one can snatch them away from me**

6. Ask anything. **John 14:12,13 In solemn truth I tell you, anyone believing in me shall do the same miracles (works) I have done, and even greater ones, because I am going to be with the Father. You can ask Him for *anything,* using my name, and I will do it, for this will bring praise and glory to the Father because of what I, the Son, will do for you. Yes, ask *anything, using my name*, and I will do it!**

7. <u>Your creator gives you life!</u> **John 12:44 Jesus said "If you trust me, you are really trusting God. For when you see me, you are seeing the one who sent me. I have come as a Light to shine in this dark world, so that all who put their trust in me will no longer wander in the darkness. I know His instructions lead to eternal life so whatever He tells me to say, I say"**

CHAPTER THREE

2Chronicles 7:14 "Pray and seek My Face".

SEEKING GOD'S FACE

Seeking the face of God is to have the desire to know God's heart, His Will, His characteristics, His faithfulness, and to experience His unconditional love. One way we come to know God is through His written Word, the Bible. Another is through the power of the Holy Spirit. In His Word we can see His character, personality, sense of humor, and His abundant love for us. We also learn about ourselves, our propensities, weaknesses, strengths, etc.. from God's perspective. Through the Holy Spirit we can hear His voice deep within our soul (telling us this is the way, walk in it), and feel His presence with every being of our existence.

Like all children we, too, need to know our limits and boundary lines that our heavenly Father has set for us. If you truly want to seek and know God, study His Word and pray for God to reveal Himself to you and He will. Be ready to obey all of what He tells you to do. Jesus said: **John 14:23 "I will only reveal myself to those who love me and obey me. The Father will love them too, and we will come to them and live with them. Anyone who doesn't obey Me doesn't love Me." Psalm 86:11 "Teach me your way, O Lord, and I will walk in your truth; give me an undivided heart". John 14:26 "The Holy Spirit will teach you much."**

God knows our hearts, and when you are ready to Know your creator, God Jehovah, God of the universe, God who is the beginning and the end, God of the Holy Bible, all you need to do is ask Him to come into your heart. You must, come to Him with a pure and willing heart. This means a heart purged from sin through repentance, of all known and unknown sins. **Psalms 24:4 He who has clean hands** and a pure heart, who has not lifted himself up to falsehood or to what is false, nor sworn deceitfully. **Matthew 5:8** **Blessed are the pure in heart: for they shall see God.** When you experience the love of God, you will experience a love so deep, powerful, and intense that it becomes almost impossible to describe or articulate your experience to others. Only your spirit can relate this kind of supernatural joy in response to the Holy Spirit, as our natural mind knows no words to explain this extraordinary phenomena that resonates deep within our soul.

God's love for us is so miraculous, that He actually sacrificed His only Son so we could have a way back to Him, and also, have a personal relationship with Him! Jesus Christ was the blood sacrifice, that was required for the atonement of sin and reconciliation to God. This kind of love staggers the imagination; It is impossible for the human mind to even begin to understand the depth of His love for us. If we could totally comprehend God's kind of love, we would be a faithful and obedient people to Him. At ball games, we would often see signs with **John 3:16** written on them, which says, **"For God so loved the world, that He gave His only begotten Son, that whosoever believeth in Him should not perish, but have everlasting life."**

God is good and His love is evident in the goodness of people; and when we witness them demonstrating their concern, compassion, empathy, kindness and unconditional love to total strangers, we have then seen the face of God. Jesus Christ commands us in, **John 15:12** **("This is My commandment, that you love one another, just as I have loved you.")** to love one another. Notice He commands us to love not judge, persecute or hate. We can love someone and not condone a lifestyle or behavior. We don't embrace sin but Jesus wants us to embrace the opportunity to love one another, just as He did. When you have a hunger and thirst for God, He will show His face in many of life's situations, but only when your heart is ready to seek.

When you worship God, that is to give Him praise, glory, thanks and live in accordance with His commands, you will then feel the intensity of His love and presence. This will be so profound and penetrating that you will never want to leave His side again. **Nehemiah 1:5** **"O great and awesome God who keeps His promises and is so loving and kind to those who love and obey Him"** **Psalms 139:2-3** **"I face your Temple as I worship, giving thanks to you for all your loving kindness and your faithfulness,**

for your promises are backed by all the honor of your name. When I pray, you answered me, and encourage me by giving me the strength I need." In just a few words from Scripture, we know God is great and awesome. He keeps His promises, He is loving and kind, He is faithful, He is a giver of encouragement and strength, and He is our provider. Imagine how much more you will know Him, when you read the letters (Holy Bible) He wrote to you! As you are reading the Bible, the Holy Spirit will open yours eyes and heart so you can see God and know His Truth!

CHAPTER FOUR

> 1Corinthians 2:10 "God revealed these things by His Spirit. For His Spirit searches out everything and shows us God's deep secrets. Amos 4:13 "The Lord reveals His thoughts to mankind. Isaiah 43:12 "I have revealed and saved; declares the Lord, "that I am God

GOD REVEALED

Compassion and mercy:

Compassion quickly comes to mind when describing God's characteristics. When we come to know God our spiritual eyes are opened and we see His sweet compassionate love all around us. It was never God's intent that we struggle, and stumble, and flounder about helplessly like a fish on a hook. If God's *Will* were being done, the world would look very different to what we have now. The absence of God's *Will* is evident in the current condition of the world, and rebellion against God is clearly demonstrated with the growing evilness. Even with this defiance, God still shows love, and compassion, and mercy for His people.

Think of a child that disobeyed his parents and found himself in a difficult predicament that could have costly consequences if left to his own devices. It's when the parent shows mercy and compassion that frees him and gives him the opportunity to correct his errors, with hopes of a mindset and behavior change. Without mercy and compassion from his parents his consequences could be an unfavorable life change or even death.

We all need the mercy of God on our lives if we are to have any hope of a long and prosperous life. Just think of the many things in your own life such as a near miss car accident, or some other near miss that could have turned out horrible if it had not been for Gods mercy and His compassion for you. Even when we make a poor decision and find ourselves in harms way, He will still show us an escape route or open another door that He can gently nudge us through.

Because of Gods love and compassion for us, He makes Himself available to us twenty-four seven. We may call on Him anytime, anywhere, for any reason, and He will hear our call without fail, He is our God, and our Creator.

Exodus 33:19 **The Lord said, "I will have mercy on whom I will have mercy, and I will have compassion on whom I will have compassion."** **Psalm 103:8** **"The Lord is compassionate and gracious, slow to anger, abounding in love".**

Patience:

God is very patient with us and this is a blessing beyond measure. Do you remember when you were taught to tie your shoes? Do you remember how many times you had to try again and again to get that shoe tied while your teacher patiently stood by ready to help until you got it right and finally you learned? Think of how proud and excited you were. Now imagine if God didn't have patience with us, what would happen. Would our life be over before it got started? Just think of the patience He must have for those of us who insist on doing things our own way and we get it wrong so many times.

Patience is something God will teach us and it can be a tough lesson to learn. God wants us to be patient with others as He is with us, for when we display patience to others, we show them God's patience and love. The Lord will allow many circumstances in our lives that require us to have much patience. This is how He teaches us. You can't have patience without first trusting in God. It is the trust in God that gives us the assurance and peace that He is in control, so we can wait upon the Lord with confidence that He is forever working on our behalf, working for what is best for us. Fear not, God will give us numerous opportunities to practice patience; actually more than we want. The patience and trust test will be given to us time and time again. **Romans 15:5** **"Now may the God of patience and comfort grant you to be like minded toward one another, according to Christ Jesus."**

It's the devil who encourages us with the hurry up technique, so we won't take the time to pray or think about the decision we are about to make. We have all seen this same method used on television commercials and infomercials. You know, the ones that say if you call within the next 10 minutes . . . , they use it for the same reason, so you won't really think about it. When God gives you a thought, idea, or nudge, He gives you plenty of time to pray about it and to test the spirits, as He tells us to do.

Fortunately for us, our Lord is patient enough with us to let us fall, and He patiently waits for us to get up, and when we fall again, He waits for us to get up again. He continues to wait, until we are ready to move forward with Him. He knows exactly what you need, and He remembers every promise He has given you, All you need to do is wait for his perfect timing and every promise will come to pass. Learn to trust Him and patience will follow. **Psalm 37:7 "Be still before the Lord and wait patiently for Him."**

Sensitivity:

God is sensitive and He is sensitive to our needs. As always, he has an unlimited amount of understanding of our forever changing moods. He is aware of and responsive to our feelings and the feelings of others. He never hesitates to correct us when we are wrong and yet, He will not condemn us. His corrections are always done in love, and at the same time He will encourage us to stay on His path. When you cry out to Him, He will extend his hand of help and safety and you will know His sweet fragrance and tender presence close to you.

When God touches your life, and calls your name, and gently whispers for you to trust Him, your heart will leap with joy and your spirit will shout, He knows my name and He knows me, He really does care! This experience will change your life forever. No one can ever touch your heart the way God can.

When you become sensitive to God's calling you, to Him, you will hear His voice speaking to your spirit and you will understand what He is saying to you. Be still and listen and know that God is who He says He is. Listen with your spiritual ears to that voice deep inside of you. In the book of **Isaiah 48: the Lord said "I clearly told you what was going to happen in the future. For I am God—I only and there is no other like me" #30 "you will hear a Voice (God) behind you" #50 the Lord said *"Listen to me" #43*

The Lord said "I have called you by name; you are mine." #59 Listen now! The Lord isn't too weak to save you. And He isn't getting deaf! He can hear you when you call!"

You get the idea, you do have the ability to hear God and He does hear you. Sometimes one needs to exercise the skill of listening to Him, but the power and sensitivity is within you.

Protection:

Protection from the Lord is directly related to our obedience to the Lord and our faithfulness. You may be protected by the Lord over hundreds of times in a day, without you ever knowing about it. Then there are the times you are very much aware of His protection. **Isaiah 58 :8** . . . **goodness will be a shield before you, and the glory of the Lord will protect you from behind. Then, when you call, the Lord will answer, "Yes, I am here" He will quickly reply.**

When we were growing up our earthly father had rules in place for our protection. Even though, as a child, we didn't understand it was for our best, when we became an adult we could see the reasoning behind the rule. Our Heavenly Father has rules and principles that must be followed for our own protection. When the rules are broken there is a natural consequence to be paid. That consequence could be something as small as a disappointment to something as drastic as death. God makes it pretty clear, to each of us, what will happen if we choose disobedience over obedience to Him.

I remember some years back we had many days of a hard winter ice, snow then rain. Needless to say this brought much flooding in many areas of my hometown. People were sandbagging their yards, garages and all areas that led to their homes. I went outside and stood on my deck, and it was like standing on a dock. I even had ducks floating in my back yard. I went back inside the house and stood in my computer room, which was the lowest point of the house, as I was trying to decide how to get all the computer cords off the ground, for safety, it was that very moment, I heard the Lord speak to me loud and clear, "If you move one single cord up off the floor I will not protect your home from the flood waters, as you will be showing Me you do not trust Me." I just stood there staring at the floor and all of those cords. I knew then that I had to make a choice;

trust the Lord or respond to what I see in front of me. I walked out of the room saying okay Lord I am putting my trust in you.

The next day, I was at my work place, when my son called and asked me if I had flood insurance, and the he told me my neighborhood was flooded. After I hung up, I went down the hall and grabbed my prayer partner and off to the chapel we went. We sent out some heavy duty prayers, that day and I think we reminded God of every promise He ever made. This called for some serious praying! After praying I went home, and had to park my car about a block or so away from my house because of high water. My home was totally surrounded by water, that's front, back and sides. I had to wade through the water to get to my house. I went in the house and noticed I was soaked from the knees down. I just stood there in the entry way not knowing what to do. I couldn't tell, by looking, if the carpet was wet, so I got down on my hands and knees to feel the carpet, and it was bone dry! I ran to the computer room and it was bone dry, not one drop of water was on the floors. I looked down and saw how wet I was and said out loud, "oh Lord look how wet I am" and that same Voice that told me not to pick up the computer cords, said "I didn't say I would keep *you* dry". God with a sense of humor!! Obedience brought protection. All the other homes on my street were flooded and my home was nearest to the lake. It felt like a double edge sword, I was extremely grateful for God's protection of my home, but I felt awful for my neighbors that were flooded.

This is not to say we shouldn't be wise and do all we know what to do in a crisis, but we should ask God for His wisdom. In this particular situation God used the circumstance to teach me a lesson in obedience and trust. Deep in my spirit, God gave me the impression of what I was to do or not do and the consequence if I did not obey. I didn't have the thought to test the spirit, I just prayed, "Lord this is what I believe you are telling me to do, (then I repeated to God what I believed He told me) if this is not true please correct me, in Jesus name amen". The belief of what God wanted me to do was so very strong that I knew I had to obeyed what the Holy Spirit was revealing to me or else!

Sometimes God will allow bad things to happen to get us back on the right path. The importance of daily communication with God brings us His guidance, instructions and teachings. Once you have declared God, our Lord of the Holy Bible, as your God, He will do whatever it takes to keep you safe and close to Him. It's a fulltime job protecting us, as the enemy, Satan, is doing all he can to get us away from God one way or another.

It is not realistic of anyone to expect protection from their enemy, is it? But that is exactly the expectations of people who want protection from the very God, they choose not to love, or believe, or worship or follow. Some think our God of the Holy Bible will bless and protect all, regardless of their alliances or bond. I can assure you, this is not the Lord's teaching. It is true, God loves all humans as His love is unconditional. However, His blessings, favor, protection, and salvation is conditional and it belongs to those who Love and obey God, and the unbelievers will be left to their own devices or their own god, whatever that might be. Of course, the door is always open for the unbeliever to repent and accept Jesus Christ as their Lord and Savior.

When Jesus was praying to our Heavenly Father, He asked that . . . . **John 17:15 "I am not asking you take them out of the world, but to keep them safe from Satan's power." also for future believers." Hebrews 13:5 God has said "I will never, _never fail_ you nor forsake you."**

Faithfulness:

It is such a comfort to know we have one source on the face of the earth that is one hundred percent faithful, reliable, true to one's word, truthful, trustworthy, loyal and committed. Our Holy God is the *only source* we can truly depend on, and believe. You see, it is impossible for God to lie, therefore, everything He says and every promise He makes to you, He must do. Our virtues or lack of; does not determine God's faithfulness. **Hebrews 6:17-18 "God also bound Himself with an oath, so that those He promised to help would be perfectly sure and never need to wonder whether He might change His plans. He has given us both His promise and His oath, two things we can completely count on, for it is impossible for God to tell a lie."**

All of us have experienced or know someone who was hurt from empty promises and painful lies. Some just can't recover from the devastation of unfaithfulness and the sorrow of their disappointments and being deceived. Rest assured, God will never be the one to bring these wounds upon us. Who, other than God, can make such promises? **Romans 3:3 "Because they broke their promises to God, does that mean God will break His promises? Of course** not! Though everyone else in the world is a liar, God is not. God's words will always prove true and right, no matter who questions them."

No matter what your story is, and we all have one, one thing is for sure, God can and will change your future and you can depend on His loyalty, protection and love to change you. He will give you, a new you for your new life! **Ephesians 4:23, 24** "..to be made new in the attitude of your minds; and to put on the new self, created to be like God in true righteousness and holiness."

Forgiveness:

If God were not a merciful and a forgiving God, there would be no purpose for our life; since none of us would or ever could be perfect without sin. We would be doomed to be Satan's property. It's because of God's forgiving heart and love for us that He unselfishly sent His sinless Son to die for our sins! Jesus took our sins of past, present and future, and put them on His life as though He were the one who sinned instead of us. The penalty for sin is death and that is why Jesus had to die, His crucifixion was the payment for our sin. **Ephesians 1:7 "So overflowing is His kindness towards us that He took away all our sins through the blood of His Son."** God knew, because of Satan's presence in this world, that it would be impossible for us to live without sin. Every single time we ask God to forgive us, He will, because that is His nature. **Hebrews 8:12 "And I will be merciful to them in their wrongdoings, and I will remember their sins no more."** As long as we keep repenting, He will keep forgiving and eventually, through God's mercy and the power of Jesus Christ's shed blood, we will conquer our sin and find victory to yet another area of our life where sin had found its way in. **1 John 1:9 "If we confess our sins, He is faithful and just and will forgive us of our sins and purify us from all unrighteousness."**

God wants us to forgive others just as He has forgiven us, actually, it's a little more than *wants us to,* its conditional that we do so. **Matthew 6:14 "If you forgive those who sin against you, your heavenly Father will forgive you. But if you refuse to forgive others, your Father will not forgive your sins."**

CHAPTER FIVE

ISAIAH 59:2 "Your iniquities have separated you from your God; your sins have hidden His face from you, so that He will not hear.**

SURRENDER ALL TO GOD

Before we were born we lived in heaven with our Heavenly Father. We were sent to earth to make a choice, we could either choose our heavenly Father's eternal plan for us or Satan's eternal plan. Therefore, God gave us, at birth, a free will, so we would have the freedom to make our own choice. Satan, as well, came from heaven. **Luke 10:18 Jesus said, "I was watching Satan fall from heaven like lightning.** As of today, Satan has access to God, but this will end when Jesus returns to earth to collect His followers and the Holy spirit, and then heaven's door will be closed, leaving behind non believers of God and Jesus Christ and Satan and his demons. At this time the earth will be void of the Holy Spirit and access to heaven will not longer exist. **1 Thessalonians 4:16-17 For the Lord Himself will descend from heaven with a shout, with the voice of the archangel and with the trumpet of God, and the dead in Christ will rise first. Then we (Christ Followers) who are alive and remain will be caught up together with them in the clouds to meet the Lord in the air, and so we shall always be with the Lord.**

In the meantime, God sent His Son Jesus with a map (Holy Bible) for us to find our way back to heaven. Satan, on the other hand, will do everything in his power to keep us from finding our way back to God. Until heaven's door is closed, Satan has to get permission from God to tempt us, but he cannot kill us. Every evil thing, thought and act comes from Satan, as he is void of good.

Satan is the father of lies, he is the destroyer, he is the darkness of earth. **Job 1:6 One day the angels came to present themselves before the Lord, and Satan the Accuser came with them.** Satan told God the only reason God's servant Job was so good and faithful was the fact God had bless him so richly. **Job 1:11 But take away everything he has, and he will surely curse you to your face! "All right, you may test him," the Lord said to Satan. "Do whatever you want with everything he possesses, but don't harm him physically." So Satan left the Lord's presence.**

Surrendering our Will and life to God, is to acknowledge God Jehovah is our creator and Jesus Christ is the only Son of God, who lived, died on the cross for our sins, He rose one the third day. When we surrender, we come into covenant with God and we choose to love, obey and worship our Him. We put God first in our lives and everything we think or do. **Hebrews 11:6 "Anyone who wants to come to God must believe that there is a God and that He rewards those who sincerely look for Him." Romans 10:10-13 "For it is in believing in his heart that a man becomes right with God; and with his mouth he tells others of his faith, confirming his salvation. Jew and Gentile are the same in this respect: they all have the same Lord who generously gives His riches to all those who ask Him for them. Anyone who calls upon the Lord will be saved."** No one can surrender our Will to the Lord, for us. Each individual must take a stand. Our friends, family, children, parents or church, absolutely no one, can make this covenant for us, this is solely our choice. If you make the decision not to make a choice; then your choice is for Satan.

Satan is the master of lies and the popular lie, of his today, is "there are many ways to heaven," there is NOT. There are many, of what the world calls "good people," who reject Jesus Christ as their Lord and savior, that will not make it back to heaven. God gave us a specific pathway that we must follow, without exception, and that path is Jesus Christ. **John 14:6 Jesus said, "I am the way, the truth, and the life. No one can come to the Father except through me."** Satan has tons of lies he puts in our heads. Such as, the bible isn't literal or the bible isn't translated correctly, giving us the option to pick and choose or believe or not believe whatever, Scriptures suits us best. Another one is, its too late for you, God can't forgive your screw ups. or God loves everyone, but you. Here is a popular and misleading lie, God loves and forgives everyone so don't worry about it, or I am a good person so I don't need to worry about that stuff. When you live like the devil wants you to live, when does God forgive you? You may only have ten minutes left on this earth, you don't know, meanwhile, you have already made the choice to go with Satan. Satan will continue to deceive until the end of time, that's his nature. He uses a little truth mixed in with his lies to convince you that his lie is truth. Protect yourself, know your enemy.

Aside from those who believe Satan's lies, there are many who simply don't know how to surrender or they have the conviction they must get their life in order first. Years ago there used to be a party called *come as you are.* The host would call a person to come to the, *as you are party,* and usually the phone calls would come late at night so people would show up in pajamas or hair in rollers and no make up, well, you get the idea. COME THE WAY YOU ARE, is exactly the time to come to the Lord.

To be honest, none of us are good enough to come to the Lord. He will clean us up and make us presentable before God. So, if you wait until you get your life in order, you will never surrender. The truth is, we are not capable of cleaning up our own life. We need the cleansing power of Jesus Christ. Our Lord will make all the necessary changes according to His Will and plans. We cannot change our past mistakes, either, but God will redeem us and use our mistakes for the good of His plan for us. Only God has the power and knowledge to change our inner-self to become a new creature for His kingdom, for only God can change our thoughts, desires, and soften our hearts to be in line with His Will, and only God can change us to be the person He intended for His purpose and His glory.

Along with having a new and softer heart, you will have new ears to hear Him with and new eyes to see His truth. You will hear His voice, yes, despite an unbelieving world, God will speak to you in many ways and you will follow His voice. **John 10:27-28 Jesus said, "My sheep recognize my voice and I know them and they follow me. I give them eternal life and they shall never perish. No one shall snatch them away from Me for My Father has given them to Me, and He is more powerful than anyone else, so no one can kidnap them from Me." John 8:12 Jesus said, "I am the light of the world. So if you follow me you won't be stumbling through the darkness, for living light will flood your path."**

The secular (unbelieving) population has the mindset that Christians should be perfect in every way. This of course, is a ridiculous expectation. Unfortunately, too many Christians try to live up to these expectations, and when they fail, the secular people are quick to label them as hypocrites. As long as we live in this world of evil, that Satan patrols, we will always fall short. That's why Jesus did what He did on the cross, so we could repent and have another chance. It is inevitable that Christians will sin, and that's why we are so grateful for God's mercy and grace. Jesus Christ is the only person ever to live in this evil world, and not sin. If we were capable of not sinning there would have been no need for Jesus to die for us. Fortunately, those who choose to surrender to our Lord will experience the "rebirth" or "born again", meaning made new in Christ. Even though we live in a sinful world, Christians do have the responsibility to live the way Jesus has instructed us. We may not be perfect but we can live perfectly.

When we are born again in the Spirit of Jesus Christ, it is His blood that washes away our filthy sins. He makes us white and pure as the virgin snow. This washing gives Jesus a new and pure canvas to do His miracle work in us. **Corinthians 5:17 "When someone becomes a Christian he becomes a brand new person inside. He is not the same anymore. A new life has begun!" John 3:3-18 Jesus declared, "I tell you the truth, no one can see the kingdom of God unless he is born again." "Flesh gives birth to flesh, but the Spirit gives birth to spirit." For God did not send His Son into the world to condemn the world, but to save the world through Him. Whoever believes in Him is not condemned, but whoever does not believe stands condemned already because He has not believed in the name of God's one and only son."**

Surrendering to the Lord is a commitment and desire to be obedient, and to do the Lord's Will and not your own. A simple prayer, in your own heartfelt words, will move the hand of God on your life. **Surrender Prayer:** *Our Holy Father in heaven, I come to you in the name of our Lord Jesus Christ. Lord, I surrender my free will and life to you. Father, I pray you will change my heart and life to reflect your love. I am your servant, Lord, use me as you will. Change my heart to be like yours, Lord. I love and worship you and I praise you Lord. Thank you for choosing me to serve and love you. Amen* **Sinners Prayer:** *Father God, I come to you in the name of our Lord Jesus Christ. I ask you to forgive me, as I* *have sinned against you. I believe Jesus Christ is the only Son of God. I believe He died on the cross for our sins. I believe He rose from the dead on the third day and is seated at the right hand of the Father. I believe Jesus is alive and will come again. I believe Jesus is my Lord and Savior and I ask Him into my heart today. In Jesus' name. Amen*

CHAPTER SIX

Philippians 4:6 **Do not be anxious about anything, but in everything, by prayer and petition, with thanksgiving, present your requests to God.**

HOW TO PRAY

How to pray to God could be summed up in three words: **from the heart**! Jesus put it this way in the book of **Matthew 6:5-8** **"And now about prayer. When you pray, don't be like the hypocrites who love to pray publicly on street corners and in the synagogues where everyone can see them. I assure you that is all the reward they will ever get. But when you pray, go away by yourself, shut the door behind you, and pray to your Father secretly. Then your Father, who knows all secrets, will reward you. "When you pray, don't babble on and on as people of other religions do. They think their prayers are answered only be repeating their words again and again. Don't be like them, because your Father knows exactly what you need even before you ask Him!**

Don't be afraid to let God know what is truly in your heart and mind. God wants His people to be happy and enjoy the best life on earth that He designed for you. God created everyone, but for those who surrender their lives to Him, God becomes their Heavenly Father, who loves them with all His heart, and He will also be your friend and counselor through the Holy Spirit. God will not chastise or condemn us for what we reveal to Him, however, when you repent, He will put you on the path He has made for you, so you may experience all the good things He has for you.

We parents know what it is like to want to do every good thing for our children and give them every advantage to be happy and successful. It is our desire to love and protect our children from every evil and harmful situation, and it is our hope our children will feel safe enough to come to us for advice or help with a problem when they need it. **Matthew 7:11 If you then, being evil, know how to give good gifts to your children, how much more will your Father who is in heaven give good things to those who ask Him!** Not to bring God down to our level, but that is what He desires of us. David is talking to God in **Psalms 8:3-6 "When I look up into the night skies and see the work of your fingers-the moon and the stars you have made—I cannot understand how you can bother with mere puny man, to pay any attention to him! And yet you have made him only a little lower than the angels, and placed a crown of glory and honor upon his head. You have put him in charge of everything you made; everything is put under his authority"**

To be loved so much by God, gives us the freedom to confide in Him with pure trust and love. Just knowing He is not going to condemn us, but has a desire to help us, all because Jesus opened the door for us to approach God's Holy throne. **Hebrews 4:16 So let us come boldly to the throne of our gracious God. There we will receive His mercy, and we will find grace to help us when we need it most.** We don't need to worry about asking the wrong things as the Holy Spirit will help us in our praying. **Romans 8:26 By faith the Holy Spirit helps us with our praying. For we don't know how to pray as we ought. But the Spirit Himself makes intercession for us with groaning which can't be uttered.** God hears and answers all prayers of His righteous ones. He may not always answer the way we think He should, but He will always answer for what is good and best for us individually.

Even though our Heavenly Father loves and adores us, we still need to approach our God with reverence and respect. We must always be mindful He is a Holy, Holy God that we serve, and He deserves our praise, honor and respect. We bow before our God because He is Holy and we love Him. He is not the "man up stairs" or the "hey bro" or any other disrespectful slang. He is our heavenly Father.

Jesus does give us guidelines in praying. We must come in faith, for its faith that moves the hand of God. We ask God to forgive us, but first we must forgive others so God can forgive us. We give Him praise and thanks for all He has done and glorify His Holy name, for **everything good** comes from God. When we pray, we ask in the name of Jesus Christ for Jesus said in **John 14:13** **"You can ask Him for anything, using My name, and I will do it, for this will bring praise to the Father because of what I, the Son, will do for you. Yes, ask *anything*, using my name, and I will do it!"** You must be sure not to ask amiss or with doubt or your prayers will go unanswered. **James 4:3** **You ask, and receive not, because you ask amiss, that you may consume it upon your lusts.** Now in your own words tell your heavenly Father what is on your heart. Be specific in exactly what you want or need God to do. Talk with Him the way you would your very best friend. Let Him know why you want or need this prayer. Pour your heart out, the Holy Spirit will help you. End your prayer in the Name of Jesus Christ. When you pray in faith, you will give God thanks before you see your answered prayer, in the natural. Have great faith!

It's also important that we pray for others and their needs, and pray for our country that God will grant the leaders wisdom, strength, courage, and fairness. **Matthew 6"9-13** **Jesus said to pray like this: "Our Father in heaven, may your name be kept holy. Let your kingdom come. Let your will be done on earth, as it is in heaven. Give us today our daily bread. Forgive our debts, as we forgive our debtors. Bring us not into temptation, but deliver us from evil. For yours is the kingdom, the power, and the glory forever. Amen**

CHAPTER SEVEN

Mark 11:23 "anyone does not doubt in his heart but believes that what he says will happen, it will be done for him.

WHAT IS FAITH and HOW TO OBTAIN IT

For most adults, faith is a process, but for most children faith is instant. When you tell your child you will take him/her to the candy store, your child instantly believes with all his heart, that *promise* will come true. Young children have open hearts filled with trust and they have open minds that lack doubt. They believe what we tell them with no reservations. Faith, like love is a decision we make to trust and believe our Lord. Jesus tells us we must come to Him like a child. With the same belief, trust and love as a child. **Luke 18:16, 17, Jesus said "let the children come to me. Don't stop them! For the Kingdom of God belongs to such as these.. I assure you, anyone who doesn't have their kind of faith will never get into the Kingdom of God."**

Every time a parent breaks his promise, a little bit of trust is torn away from that child's heart. Promise breaking will eventually teach a child not to believe, not to trust, and fill their minds with doubt. The child that has been lied to, will become the adult that has a difficult time believing that his Heavenly Father is different than his earthly father. Our earthly father should mirror our Heaven Father, and in a perfect world this would be true. Our Heavenly Father will hold parents accountable for the, so called, "little white lies", they have told to their children. The same is true of a child that has had been abandoned or who had an absentee father; as an adult, he/she will believe our Heavenly Father will also abandon them, in time. The flip side is, the child who had a loving and trusting-honest earthly father or father figure, has a greater belief system for trusting and believing our Heavenly Father. It is for this reason that our earthly father or father figure is so vital for a child's healthy development, for it is our nature to equate our earthly father with our Heavenly Father. It is the word "father" that we actually identify with. We have a Heavenly Father not a heavenly mother but this is in no way, to take away the importance or necessity of a child needing a nurturing loving mother.

In the Bible, the book of Luke tells us faith is a requirement for heaven so regardless of our own belief system or history, we need to learn how to grow in our faith. In the Bible the book of Hebrews gives us a clear definition of faith, so we need not be confused of what faith is. **HEBREWS 11:1 & 6 What is faith? It is the confident assurance that what we hope for is going to happen. It is the evidence of things we cannot yet see. . . . . . . You see, it is impossible to please God without faith. Anyone who wants to come to Him must believe that there is a God and that He rewards those who sincerely seek Him.** We have a hope, even though we can't see any evidence in what we are believing and hoping for, is faith. This, of course, would mean we all have some measure of faith, because we all hope for something.

I believe God has placed the seed of faith within us at the time of birth, which can develop or remain dormant. The very instinct to survive is hope, remove the hope and death will occur. A newborn will cry from instinct or hope that someone will take care of his needs. The newborn will not consciously think, *I'll cry for help*, any more than we think about taking our next breath. Nonetheless, every time that newborn's needs are met his/her faith seed grows and with consistency, he becomes quite confident that someone will take care of him. So it is with us, every time we believe and hope for something and it comes to pass, our faith seed grows, and our trust develops.

The questions are, who are you trusting, and who are you believing in, and what is your hope? Just because of what you hope for, comes to pass, does not mean it came from God. The enemy of God, Satan, will be happy to help you get what you hope for, as long as it is against God's word and is not God's plan for your life. Consciously or sub-consciously we can, also, force things to happen for us and claim its from God, when, in fact it may not be God's plan, at all. This is another reason why it is vital that we read the Word of God often, so we will know His plan and what is right. If we don't know what God tells us in His Written Word, the enemy will not have a problem leading us down the wrong path full of his lies, instead of God's truth. We must always be mindful of the enemy's objective. Satan's mission is to destroy all things created by God, especially humans. God's Word will help in protecting you from Satan's tricks and lies.

God will give us numerous opportunities to develop our faith muscle. Everyday of your life you will have, yet another chance to grow that muscle. Just as we exercise our physical muscles we need to exercise our faith muscle. Every opportunity given to us will prepare us for success when our testing times come and they will come. No test, no growth, for its in the testing our growth occurs. Learn to trust God for absolutely everything, for you will need every ounce of faith for the times you are pinned against the wall and you feel like the life is being sucked out of you and there is no hope except the hand of God. It's that daily faith muscle exercise that delivers the mega faith when you need it. Know God is on your side and wants you to succeed in every aspect of life.

Having worked in the medial field for many years, I have witnessed many, only GOD moments. I heard doctors say to families, "there is no hope, there is *no way*" and I have seen God say yes there is hope and I AM the way. The truth is, God performs miracles in our lives everyday. Some, we take for granted, like breathing, seeing, hearing, walking, surviving, shelter, near accidents, well the list goes on and on of God's wonderful miracles and for the most part we give our daily miracles, little thought until they are gone. Its not that we don't appreciate all that God does for us its just we don't always recognize His help until we are in a crises. We often, only look at miracles as the unnatural, spectacular, sensational or theatrical events such as being brought back to life after pronounced dead, growing a new limb, being alive against all odds when in fact, God also uses other avenues to perform miracles, such as medical miracles, God gives the physicians the knowledge and the technology to perform HIS WILL. God uses humans to create, in HIS power, as humans only have the power and knowledge that God allows. Human life is God's miracle to mankind. Let us not take any, big or small, miracles for granted as everything good is God's gift to us.

Many years ago, I was in a situation my current home had to be sold and I had 60 days to find a new home for my son, our dog and myself. Not too many years prior to this, it was extremely difficult for women to obtain a credit card of their own let alone buy a house.! I had just gotten a job, after not working outside the home for many years. Now I had the burden of finding a house. At first I didn't think it would be that big of a problem, but it didn't take long to figure out, I was going to need a big miracle, all of my own. Most of the homes, in my price range, needed a lot of repairs and the ones that didn't need repairs, I didn't qualify for the loan. The hunt went on without success and I was running out of time. Now it was down to the wire and still no home prospects.

Knowing I was truly against the wall, my eleven year old son and I got on our knees and poured out our hearts to the Lord. We even gave Him a list of what we needed in a home, like a fenced yard for our dog, close to my son's school, three bedroom, living room with a fireplace. I told my son we must believe and not doubt, with all our hearts that God has the perfect house for us and He will give us direction. After all, Jesus did say in the book of **John 14:12-13-14** **"I tell you the truth, anyone who has faith in me will do what I have been doing. He will do even greater things than these, because I am going to the Father.**

And I will do whatever you ask in my name, so that the Son may bring glory to the Father. *You may ask me for anything in my name and I will do it."* We stood on this promise as though our lives depended on it and not once did we listen to the naysayer but instead we kept our eyes on God's promise.

The day after my son and I had prayed together, my daughter came over to my house and said, "lets go house hunting". This was my last week of hunting and then we would need to find an apartment. My daughter was driving around a neighborhood that was obviously out of my price range and I told her I could never afford any of the homes in this neighborhood and we should look elsewhere. She immediately stopped the car and said "look this house is for sale", I reiterated what I had just said, but she wouldn't listen. She just said, "mom write the phone number down and call your realtor", so I did. I called my agent and he set up appointment for the next day to view the home. He did say to me, "you do realize this home is about forty five thousand dollars out of your price range?" That was back in the day, one hundred thousand dollars was a lot of money for a house. I assured him I knew that but I just wanted to take a look. The next morning I met him at 9 o'clock at the home to view. He told me that, another party was schedule to view the home at eight o'clock but didn't show up. No one had yet seen the house, as it just went on the market, so I was the first. When I walked through the front door I instantly went into shock, figuratively speaking. The house was exactly what my son and I prayed for. Three bedrooms, huge fenced back yard, behind the house was a beautiful park with a duck pond, soccer field, playground. The house was close to my son's school and four blocks from our church. The only thing it had wood stove prep instead of a fireplace. It was beautiful. After viewing the house, my agent and I were standing in the living room when he asked me what did I think and do your want to give an offer? I went immediately into prayer. Oh God, please help me, what do I say, help me Lord. The number 55 kept coming to mind, over and over. Finally, when the agent asked again, I blurted out 55! He looked at me as if I had three heads, and repeated, 55? He said he would present my offer but for me not to get my hopes up for "you are about forty thousand short." The next evening he had an appointment with the sellers to present my offer. He called me after their meeting and said, "I could live to be hundred and still not understand or guess what people will do. I explained to them your situation and what you could afford. They asked me to step outside and a few minutes later they asked me to come back into the house and told me they would accept your offer! They will put in new drain pipes and new bathroom floor, if you would do the painting to the outside of the house". I knew God put it on their hearts to take the offer. They had no reason to take that offer, after all they just put it on the market and they were asking ninety five thousand, plus they didn't even live there. My agent just kept saying over and over, "I don't get it, I just don't get it". I do, it's a *God thing,* and this is how faith and trust grows and grows.

It's not unlike God to allow things in our lives, to give us, our faith building *God experiences,* meaning something that happens to us or for us, that we know, without a doubt, could not have happened if it were not for God's hand of favor. When you go through rough times and some horrendous situations, it will be in those times that you will draw on all those past, *God experiences,* to get you through your current challenge. The Holy Spirit will remind you of God's past faithfulness to you. He will assure you, God does not take you down a particular path just to pull the rug out from under you. It is God's faithfulness and consistency that will keep you grounded in faith.

It is difficult to explain faith, because its not, so much, a mind thing as it is a soul experience. To believe something with all your heart and soul, without evidence, is truly a God thing. Faith must be experienced to appreciate the power in believing God and totally trust and rely on Him. Young children are much better at this then adults, for they lack history, and their hearts are, so. opened to our creator.

It's difficult to explain faith, because you just know, without reason. It's more than a feeling or intuition, its like a truth of knowledge, you just know and that is a *God thing.* Know the Word of God, Believe the Word of God, speak the Word of God, hear the Word of God, receive the Word of God and you have a recipe for faith. **Romans 10:17 "So then faith comes by hearing, and hearing by the Word of God." 1Corinthians 2:5 that your faith should not be in the wisdom of men but in the power of God. Matthew 21:21 Jesus said "Truly, I say to you, if you have faith and do not doubt, you will not only do what has been done to the fig tree, but even if you say to this mountain, Be taken up and thrown into the sea, it will happen."** What are you saying to your mountain? Everyday of our lives God will give us opportunities to know and trust Him and to stay in faith. Let God's promises give you hope, faith and direction. Live by faith, all of the time and give God a free hand to direct your life. The enemy brings trials and temptation into our lives and God will sometimes allows it so we can learn, be corrected or for us to see how much faith we have. Your faith is how you win, you will overcome the test by your faith. It's not what God *can* do for you but what you believe God *will* do for you. God will not withhold His comfort from you, but you will know God in the mist of your suffering, you only need to know who's name to call on and that would be the name of Jesus.

Heads up, the greater your faith the less pain and suffering you'll endure because you will know God has allowed the circumstance to get you where you need to be, to bring His plan for you to fruition.

Faith is our weapon to use against the enemy of God. Faith is our declaration or announcement that moves the hand of God on our behalf and it is by faith that we give obedience to God. The Book of James tells us that faith without works is dead. In other words, we must do all we can do in our humanness, that God has told us to do, and then step aside and allow God to do His work.

Faith in any other god or persons or things will stop the hand of God and bring unfavorable consequences. We trust, praise and worship only our creator God Jehovah, God of the Holy Bible, God of Abraham, Isaac and Jacob and we ask all things in the name of His only Son, our Savior Jesus Christ's name. **James 2:26 For just as** the body without the spirit is dead, so also faith without works is dead. 4:3-7 You do not have because you do not ask. You ask and don't receive because you ask with wrong motives, so that you may spend it on your evil desires. Therefore, submit to God. But resist the Devil and he will flee from you. Draw near to God, and He will draw near to you.

Commit to the Lord and live by faith and God will bless and prosper you. Read all of Proverbs 3 and be blessed.

CHAPTER EIGHT

Romans 11:22 "God is both kind and severe.
He is severe toward those who disobeyed, but kind to you if you continue to trust in His kindness. But if you stop trusting, you also will be cut off."

HOW WE STOP GOD'S BLESSINGS

God has unlimited blessings in store for us, and all we need to do is learn how to receive and appreciate His precious gifts. I know it seems ludicrous, but we are actually guilty of holding off or stopping our own blessings! Sometimes it's just because of our unbelief, but mostly, it's due to our self-convicting guilty sentence we have pronounced upon ourselves. Perhaps it's due to the fact that only we know the depth and ugliness of our own sins, therefore, subconsciously or consciously we feel undeserving of good things from God, so we sabotage His plan.

Because we know ourselves so well and our sinful nature, it's difficult for us to believe God could possibly love us as an individual, unconditionally, especially wanting to bless us. How strange it is we don't have a problem believing God will bless and love, unconditionally, the other guy! Satan takes great delight in reminding us of our sins, over and over, and he will tell us God's love and blessings are for the *other people* who deserve it and because we know our own sins so well, we agree with him, forgetting the other guy has sinned as well, for we are all sinners.

Other ways we stop God's blessings is through disobedience of His Word and rebellion. Disobedience is when we choose to ignore His instructions and the rebellion is when we choose to do it our own way with the arrogant belief we know better than God.

Nonetheless, it is true, God's love is unconditional and Scripture tells us, nothing or no one can stop Him from loving us, **Romans 8:38** 'Nothing can ever separate us from God's love. **Neither death nor life, neither angels nor demons, neither our fears for today nor our worries about tomorrow—not even the powers of hell can separate us from God's love"**, however, His blessings are conditional. In **Malachi 3:10 Speaking of tithe God said "if you do, I will open up the windows of heaven for you" Genesis 26:3 "If you do . . . I will be with you and bless you". Exodus 23:25 "You must serve only the Lord your God. If you do, I will bless you with food and water, and I will keep you healthy"**. These are just a few Scriptures showing blessings are conditional. God will bless who He chooses, in the way He wants, and in the time frame He decides, as He said in **Romans 9:15 "God said I show mercy to anyone I choose, and I will show compassion to anyone I choose". Romans 9:11 God chooses according to His own plan"**.

Of course, we don't deserve any of God's blessings, but this isn't about deserving, it's about God's Goodness and His awesome love, grace and forgiveness He has for us. According to God's biblical law, we deserve death, we deserve punishment, and we deserve hell, but because of God's extraordinary love for us we get forgiveness when we repent, we get God's Grace, and we get righteousness through Jesus Christ, because Jesus paid the price, for what we deserve!

Now think of all the good things you want to give your children or love ones and the many situations you have showered them with good blessings just because you love them. Now, we as sinful beings, know how to give good gifts to our children, just imagine how much more our heavenly Father, with all His holiness and wisdom, wants to give to His children! **Matthew 7:9-11 "If a child asks his father for a loaf of bread, will he be given a stone instead? If he asks for fish, will he be given a poisonous snake? Of course not! And if you hardhearted, sinful men know how to give good gifts to your children, won't your Father in heaven even more certainly give good gifts to those who ask Him for them?"**

All of us want to enjoy good health, success, prosperity, peace of mind, and joy for our children and ourselves, so its really exciting to know God wants nothing less for His children! Nonetheless, God will put blessings, He has in store for us, on hold until we get into His will. God will never bless sin, so if anyone is living a life of sin and refuses to repent, they can count on not receiving God's awesome blessings that He has planned for them. Now, on the other hand God rewards obedience.

The secular world (non believers) and the *enemies* of God, would have us believe, we need to take care of ourselves and be in charge of our own life, and we should pamper, spoil and think of ourselves first, after all, <u>we deserve it</u>. This **is** the message the world gives us everyday, through television, radio, movies, social events, schools, and media; you name it, these are the messages of our current world. When these ungodly messages go unchallenged, we allow the spirits of selfishness and the ultra ego to get a foothold in our lives, and then we become like the world. Christians lives should look very different from that of the world, and if they don't, they should be very concerned.

Take a look around and witness all the acts of pure selfishness. I actually had a patient tell me, "you better approve my drugs (narcotics), I deserve them! Unfortunately, this mindset has become the normal of today's world. People truly believe they <u>deserve</u> to have what they want, and call it their right, giving no thought of morals, right or wrong, or who could be affected by their actions. The mindset has become all about *me, me, me, I, I, I, and mine, mine, mine!* This selfishness is seen on the highways; we call it road rage, in the stores, we call it rudeness, and in the schools; we call it bullying, and selfishness has become so prevalent, we accept it as normal! **<u>Romans 12:3</u> "I say to every one of you: Do not think of yourself more highly than you ought, but rather think of yourself with sober judgment, in accordance with the measure of faith God has given you." <u>Romans 12:16</u> "Live in harmony with one another. Do not be proud, but be willing to associate with people of low position. Do not be conceited."**

All of us need to do some serious examination of our own heart and evaluation of our priorities and what we are teaching our children by our behavior. Even in today's world, children still learn from what they see their parents doing. So, regardless of what the world tells us, it is not healthy to focus on self, for it will make us physically and spiritually ill. When we place our focus on others, it brings about peace, joy, and true inner happiness, for it is the Will of God that we put the love of others before ourselves. When we focus on the welfare of others, God puts His focus on us and our needs. **<u>John 13:34</u> "A new command I give you: Love one another. As I have loved you, so you must love one another. <u>1Peter 3:8</u> "Finally,**

all of you, live in harmony with one another; be sympathetic, love as brothers, be compassionate and humble.

When our children go in the way we instructed them and they are loving and obedient, we just want to bless their socks off, and so it is with our Heavenly Father, He too, wants to bless our socks off, when we are obedient. When we read of all the blessings and promises in God's Word, we get just a glimpse of God's desire to pour His favor and blessings upon His children who love, honor and obey Him. The Bible is very clear that obedience will bring about God's favor, so if we do our part God will do His promises.

Don't allow the devil to rob you of one more single blessing by you believing his lies. Instead, receive your blessings from God with love, obedience and a grateful heart. It's a good thing, for us, that God can read our heart and not just our lip service. On the other hand, our enemy, the devil can't read your heart or your mind, but he can read your lips, your body language, and he can put thoughts in your mind and its with your mind the battles are won or lost. God has a great and wonderful plan for your life so don't let Satan ruin it, for you.

Here are just a couple of blessings listed in the Bible that God has in store for you. **Leviticus 26:10,6,9,12,44, and Deuteronomy 8:18 "You will have such a surplus that you won't know what to do..", "I will give you peace, and you will go to sleep without fear." "I will look after you".. "I will walk among you and be your God." "I am Jehovah your God" "Always remember that it is the Lord your God who gives you power to become rich, and He does it to fulfill His promises to your ancestors."** Don't stop your blessings by not trusting the one and only, God Jehovah, who loves you more than anything else, so much so that He sent and allowed His only Son to die for your sins!

G . . . . God's   **J . . . . Jesus First**
R . . . . Riches   **O . . . . Others Second**
A . . . . At   **Y . . . . You Last**
C . . . . Christ's
E . . . . Expense

CHAPTER NINE

Numbers 6:24-26 "May the Lord bless you and protect you. May the Lord smile on you and be gracious to you. May the Lord show you His favor and give you His peace."

SPEAK GOD'S BLESSINGS
Over Your Children

All we need to do is look around and see what is happening to our children in today's broken and fallen world. We must stop pretending that Satan doesn't exist, for he is snatching our children, at an alarming rate, one child at a time! Satan is the ring leader of this drug craze culture, meth labs, child pornography, child rape-molestation and child prostitution; just to name a few of his hideous, repulsive and revolting sins committed against our young children. Turning a blind eye and deaf ear is giving Satan permission to take our precious children to destroy their souls and do what he pleases. We have the power, through our Lord Jesus Christ, to stop the enemy and we must act now!

It is imperative, for our children's sake and our future, that we not only pray for our children every single day of their lives, we must lay hands on their head and speak God's promises and His Word, over them! If ever, in the history of mankind did the young ever need prayers of protection from the enemy, it is NOW! We must plead the Blood of the Lamb of God over our children for their protection, is in the Blood of Christ as is **all** power, is in the Blood of Jesus Christ. The Devil or the evil spirits, cannot touch what is covered with the blood of Christ. *My Heavenly Father, I ask in the name of our Lord, Jesus Christ, that you protect and cover (child's name)*

with the precious blood of our Lord Jesus. Jesus you said, in John 10:28 "no one shall snatch them away from me." **and in John 14:12 you said** "In solemn truth I tell you, you can ask for anything in My name, and I will do it; for this will bring praise and glory to the Father, because of what I, the Son, will do for you." **Lord, I stand on your promises and give you thanks and all the praise and glory. Amen** Jesus spilled His blood on the cross for you and me, so let us not waste this precious gift from God. Your _protection_ is in **the blood,** your _healing_ is in **the blood**, your _blessing_ is in **the blood**, your _salvation_ is in **the blood**, your _ticket home_ (heaven) is in **the blood** and Jesus Christ's **blood** is the _payment_ for our soul.

We wouldn't send our child off to school, in snowy cold weather, without giving him/her a protective covering, so why would we send our children out into the world, without the protective covering of Jesus Christ? Yet, millions of children, in today's world, are raising themselves and making adult decisions without the advantage of having adult experience and wisdom. Childhoods are being stripped away, by the thousands. Five year olds being left alone, babies being left with eight year old sitters, eleven year olds smoking, and twelve year olds and younger, dating!

Far too many parents have their own private lives and their children have their own little private lives and the two shall remain separate. Unbelievable amount of parents, have their own careers taking priority, therefore, they hire nannies, and yet others have older children to baby sit and many young children are left alone with the television or computer games to baby sit. The sad fact remains, the children are raising themselves, with their own limited knowledge as their guide! Have these parents forgotten or do they not know, that God will hold every parent responsible for the welfare of their children. These irresponsible acts by parents have certainly given Satan access to many of God's young children. All of us have the responsibility to pray for these children, even if they are not our own. We all need to pray for God's hedge of protection from predators, unworthy parents, Satan's tricks and lies, and pray for God's blessings and favor to be upon every child. We must rebuke the enemy, the devil, away from these Children! These children are the future of the world.

Children that are without discipline, guidance, godly values, love, and whose actions demonstrate lack of respect, defiance and rebellion are on their way to becoming the possession of the enemy.

Children are rebellious because they don't have the love, discipline and godly guidance they so desire and need. It's not a phase or "just being a teenager", it's a child lacking. All children need their parents *time, discipline* and *love* and without it they feel the emotional pain of loneliness, depression, unworthiness, and self-doubt. These emotional feelings will cause children to seek acceptance and love, elsewhere. It is this combination of emotions that entices young people to use drugs so they can ease their pain! It's not peer pressure that brings children to drug use, it's actually the lack of love, lack of confidence and the unmanageable emotional pain that wins them over. Neglect is a very effective tool that the enemy uses and wins his prey over. Love is not shown with material things it's shown with discipline and time and it is that, very important, *parent time, that* today's children, are robbed of. **Proverbs 13:24 If you refuse to discipline your children, it proves you don't love them; if you love your children, you will be prompt to discipline them. Proverbs 19:18 Discipline your children while there is hope. If you don't, you will ruin their lives.** The Lord is talking about correction, *NOT* abuse or cruelty, so pray for wisdom and know the difference, as the Lord says in **Malachi 2:16 "God hates . . . cruel men"**

Seventeen or eighteen years ago my daughter and son-in-law were married. They both had busy careers at a well known airlines, however, after a couple years of marriage they decided they wanted to start a family. During my daughters maternity leave she felt uncomfortable with the idea of someone else raising her child while she worked. After much prayer, she and her husband decided that my daughter would not return to her employment with the airlines, but instead would be a fulltime stay at home mother. They also knew with this decision that they would need to sacrifice buying a home, for a this time. They live a few blocks from Golden Gate Park in San Francisco, which became the children's back yard. My grandchildren spent their early years visiting many, many museums, zoos, art and science displays, they were busy everyday and television was a very limited privilege. Fifteen years later they are buying their first home and I can say with all certainty, living in a two bedroom apartment (two adults and two active boys), they learned to respect each others space and they are definitely a very close family with many rich blessings. The two boys are intelligent, well adjusted, kind, caring, happy individuals who value the true meaning of family. This is God's blessings to them, for obeying, sacrificing and being the parents He called them to be. They sacrificed material things to give the boys their time, love, discipline, and fulltime parenting. All four agree it was worth the fifteen year wait for their new home. They have a greater understanding for the meaning of respect and love for one another and the importance of waiting for God's timing, all of which, cannot be taught in the schools. My daughter is a writer and enjoys all the wonderful blessings God' has so graciously given her.

Love your future enough to bless and be a blessing to your children, grandchildren, nephew, niece, friend, or neighbor. All children need our prayers. Give a child your blessing, today. Pray: *Our Heavenly Father, thank you for (child's name). In the name of Our Lord Jesus Christ, I pray you will fill (child's name) with your wisdom and love. I pray, Lord, you will bless and light his/her path and give him/her a heart for your righteousness and truth. Put people in his/her life to help develop according to your Will.* Blessing: *Hands on child head and say (child's name)* **Numbers 6:24-26 "May the Lord bless and protect you; may the Lord's face radiate with joy because of you; May He be gracious to you; show you His favor, and give you His peace."** *Our God of Abraham, Isaac and Jacob, will bless you with plenty so you may grow to be a blessing to others, Our God will keep you in good health, mentally and physically. He will grant you with godly wisdom and He will write His word on your heart. He will bless you with an obedient heart and righteousness for His name sake. In Jesus Name. Amen* All children deserve to have these blessings said over them, and they all need our prayers of protection. We do live in a very dangerous world today, and all of us can do something to make it better. The power is in prayer! Speak positive words over your children not the curse of negativity. **Proverbs 22:6 "Teach a child to choose the right path, and when he is older he will remain upon it".**

Teach children how to love and grow in the Lord and it will bring much happiness, peace and protection to their lives and yours. Show them Christ, through you, and show them obedience through your obedience to the Lord. We can't be with our children twenty four seven, so please understand the importance that they know how to call on Jesus for help. **Isaiah 58:8 Teach your child to call upon the Lord, not to be afraid of Him."**

CHAPTER TEN

James 4:4 "if you want to be a friend of the world, you make yourself a enemy of God."

KNOW YOUR ENEMY

Like any war or battle, and this is a war, one must know his enemy and the enemy's strategies, if he wants to be victorious. Spiritual warfare is every bit as real as physical conflict or encounter. This is a war we were born into and we can't afford to lose. God and Satan are fighting for our souls; who's side are you on? Satan's goal is to destroy what God loves. His plan is to replace God! If Satan captured every soul, he still would not be able to overpower our God, and he knows this, so his plan is to keep as many souls as possible, out of heaven. Therefore, **Don't** give Satan your power, that was given to you through the Holy Spirit.

Unfortunately, too many people choose not to recognize or admit to the existence of Satan, thus, giving him an enormous amount of influence or a strong foothold over them. Denial of Satan's existence, is of course, a huge advantage for Satan to claim you as his own. Those who do not believe in his existence, have fallen for Satan's famous lie, *there is no Satan or devil*, because not believing in his existence is exactly what he wants you to think, for what better way to win! Nonetheless, denying his existence will not protect you from his influence or the many other tricks and lies he has in store for you. It is vital for Satan's success, to keep the human race in ignorance. Satan is the father of lies and his goal is to destroy the human race. **John 8:44 Jesus said "For you are the children of your father the devil and you love to do the evil things he does. He was a murderer from the beginning and a hater of truth-there is not an iota of truth in him. When he lies, it is perfectly normal; for**

he is the father of liars." Isaiah was one of God's prophets, and his role was to be a voice for God and he spoke the words that the Lord gave him to say. speaking of Satan: <u>Isaiah 14:12</u> **How you are fallen from heaven, O shining star, son of the morning! You have been thrown down to the earth, you who destroyed the nations of the world. For you said to yourself, "I will ascend to heaven and set my throne above God's stars. I will preside on the mountain of the gods far away in the north. I will climb to the highest heavens and be like the Most High." But instead, you will be brought down to the place of the dead, down to its lowest depths."** By not acknowledging the existence of Satan, is to call God a liar and to declare the Holy Bible as untrue.

Satan will put thoughts into our minds, but we have the power to entertain, accept or reject his thoughts. Satan has no power over us, unless we give it to him. Satan is well aware of our habits, history and behavior, thus, making it easy for him to plant suggestions in our minds, that will lead us to follow him. Often, he uses a very subtle and powerful technique on us, by giving us suggestions or thoughts that *seem* to be of our own. Of course that is exactly what he wants us to believe, after all, would we actually accept an idea or thought if we knew it was from the devil? His suggestions will seem logical and true to us, because he knows, by our actions and behavior, how we think.

Every time we use the word "I" or "I am, I will, I want, I can't, I won't, I have, I think", it's time to pay attention! You better back that "I" up with Scripture. It is important to Satan, that <u>we believe</u> every thought we have is our own, so he can use our mind for his battlefield. Satan is knowledgeable in human nature behavior, and that's what makes him so clever. He is well aware that our ego and arrogance of doing "our own thing", having our own way, is extremely powerful in this evil nature, this flesh of ours. Our flesh is always calling to us for some kind gratification and Satan takes advantage of every opportunity he sees. The next time you think "I" . . . be sure that the "I" is in the Will of God and not the will of Satan. Although, Satan does give outrageous, insane and evil ideas and thoughts, he mostly uses the very subtle or the gray area, if you will, until he gets his victims desensitized then he will up his game with the gross and wrong.

Satan will always be on the lookout for a foothold into our lives so, we need to be on guard at all times against his tactics. Each of knows our own weakness and it is our responsibility to protect ourselves by removing and closing the opportunities that Satan sees, to get a foothold in our lives. God, our heavenly Father has given us the tools for victory and we need to use them. Are you aware allowing yourself to overeat, be overly tired, wearing a cranky or bad disposition, and bending the truth, and anger, are just some of the bad traits of character, that will give Satan an open window. **Ephesians 4:27 for anger gives a mighty foothold to the Devil.** Satan would be more than willing to use your tiredness to get control of your mouth or to cause division in your relationships. He will take advantage of our vulnerable and weak conditions every chance he gets. He will even use food that has a over abundance of sugar, for this will bring on depression, anxiety, sleepiness, low self-esteem, self-pity, judgmental, naming just a few of the emotional maladjustments associated with chemical imbalances, just as alcohol and drugs do. Satan can do a lot of damage with what appears to be innocent, to us. Oh, what a playground, of the mind, we offer him. Now, if Satan has never used lies or any of these tactics on you, or has never given you a evil thought or has never tempted you, then you need to be very concerned because, he is telling you he doesn't need you to open a window because you already belong to him!

Satan will try to convince you that you are not valued, loved or even worthy enough to worship God so why would God waste His time with you! All he has to do is remind us of our sinful past and we get into full agreement with Him. He will use our physical appearance, "I am too fat, skinny, ugly", and emotional state, "I am stupid, selfish, worthless, unlovable, or any flaw, to convince us, that all of these negative thoughts are our own, so he can more thoroughly inflate us ; and we will be opened and accepting of him feeding us one lie after another. He will use just enough truth, in any situation, to convince us of a lie. He will also suggest to us, we are superior or inferior because of our skin color, hair color or eye color, and he will suggest we are too intelligent to buy into all that "God and Jesus stuff"; I married beneath me; my job is not good enough for me; and these are just a few of the thousands of thoughts and suggestions he fires our way, daily! The battle may start in the mind, but Satan is relentless in gaining control of our flesh. We need to use every piece of the Armor of God, **Ephesians 6:14-17 "Stand firm then, with the *belt* of truth buckled around your waist, with the *breastplate* of righteousness in place, and with your *feet fitted* with the readiness that comes from the gospel of peace.**

In addition to all this, take up the *shield* of faith, with which you can extinguish all the flaming arrows of the evil one. Take the *helmet* of salvation and the sword of the Spirit, which is the Word of God", and give God control over us, and then we may rest in His love and Security.

Satan does not want credit or acknowledgment for his work, because our ignorance will give him, far greater freedom to do his evil works in us. He has one goal, DESTROY ALL HUMANS; he hates humans and he will use any trick, deception, disaster, sex, drugs, sickness, disease, lie or any situation to accomplish his goal. Satan doesn't need us physically dead he needs us spiritually dead to gain our soul. **Peter 5:8-9 "Be careful watch out for attacks from Satan, your great enemy. He prowls around like a hungry, roaring lion, looking for some victim to tear apart. Stand firm when he attacks. Trust the Lord."** Notice it says when he attacks not if. Another technique he likes to use, is keeping us very, very busy; too busy to worship, pray or do the work the Lord has designed us to do. He will even use church work to keep us too busy! Satan will keep us so busy that we will neglect our God given responsibilities, such as family and to enjoy God and the life He gave us. If you don't know or believe Satan's plan and strategy for your life, then you will allow him to destroy your home, health, marriage, children, finances, towns, cities, country and eventually take your spirit and soul!

During crisis we often hear people say "why did God do this"? It would be rare to hear "this is the work of Satan, not of God," Of course, it is Satan's plan to have us blame God, for blaming God pleases Satan, for this gives him a opportunity to help us fail at our faith test. Plus blaming God keeps the focus off Satan freeing up open windows for the enemy to use. Furthermore, how could you rebuke something or someone you don't believe even exist? God would not have taught us how to rebuke Satan if he did not exist. **Matthew 16:23 Jesus said "Get away from me, you Satan!" Ephesians 6:10 "Your strength must come from the Lord's mighty power within you. Put on all of God's armor so that you will be able to stand safe against all strategies and tricks of Satan.: James 4:7 "So humble yourselves before God. Resist the devil and he will flee from you."**

Satan will give us a sense of urgency with decision making. His goal, of course, is to get us to make a decisions without taking it to our Lord first. He knows if we pray about it and wait for God's answer, he will lose his evil opportunity to lead us astray. The greater the importance of the decision the greater the urgency and urges we experience. This sense of urgency should be a red flag and I am not talking about medical emergency when someone needs medical care immediately, I am talking about Satan's strategy and how he is committed to get us off guard and keep us from praying to our heavenly Father. Recognize the enemy and his plan, your life depends on it. **Romans 16:20 The God of peace will soon crush Satan under your feet." 1John 3:7-8 Do not let anyone lead you astray. He who does what is right is righteous . . . He who does what is sinful is of the devil, because the devil has been sinning from the beginning.**

In the end times, we will see more and more evil in the world because Satan knows his time is short. Satan will take as many souls as he can, so don't let him have yours. **Revelation 12:12 Therefore rejoice, you heavens and you who dwell in them! But woe to the earth and the sea, because the devil has gone down to you! He is filled with fury, because he knows that his time is short".**

Satan plays the blame game and teaches us to do the same. He does not want us to admit our wrongs and sins; for he does not want us to repent for He knows God loves us so much He will forgive the truly sorry heart. Satan wants you to blame others so you will not have contrition in your heart. Satan taught Eve to blame the serpent, and Adam to blame Eve and then Adam blamed God for giving him Eve! Don't blame anyone for your actions, thoughts or behavior. Take responsibility for your actions and pray for those who do you wrong. Leave the judgment to God. You know, Satan is right now, busy accusing you, to God, telling Him how bad you are and how much you hate His Kingdom and you show it with your disobedience. So, you need to know that your Attorney and Counselor, is JESUS! That's right, Satan will do all he can to get you to listen to him and do evil and then point your evil out to God. Remember, we have only two choices in this world, we either choose God or Satan, and I tell you now, no decision made, is a choice for Satan.

Satan is a *want a be,* he wants to be God and he is frustrated because he was kicked out of heaven, the Kingdom of God, so he then set up his kingdom here on earth. Satan's kingdom on earth will only last until Jesus returns and then once and for all, He will take care of Satan and Satan's followers, forever. Don't be a Satan follower. If you are not following Jesus Christ and obeying our Lord God, you are then, a Satan follower.

So, remember Satan will talk to you often. If you are doing well he will tell you "how awesome you are and let you know that don't need anyone". especially God. He does this to build pride up in you, as he knows very well, pride will destroy you; this is why God hates pride. If you are not doing well, he will tell you "how awful and worthless you are and your life is nothing more than a display of how much God hates you"! Know the enemy and recognize his voice. Satan will say anything and do everything he can to keep you away from God. He will lie, cheat, steal, destroy, trick and know this, nothing is to wicked for him to do. Our protection is Jesus Christ! Do not fear Satan or challenge him, but take comfort in the safety of God's arms and His promises for you. **2Thessaionians 3:3** **"But the Lord is faithful; He will make you strong and guard you from the evil one."** **Colossians 2:8** **"Don't let anyone lead you astray with empty philosophy and high sounding nonsense that come from human thinking and from the evil powers of this world (9) you have everything when you have Christ. (10) He is the highest Ruler, with authority over every other power in the universe.**

CHAPTER ELEVEN

James 4:7 "humble yourselves before God. Resist the devil, and he will flee from you". **Matthew 10:8** "Heal the sick, raise the dead, cure those with leprosy, and cast out demons. Give as freely as you have received!"

REBUKE SICKNESS AND DISEASES

Rebuking sickness and disease, oh if only it were that simple. Can you imagine what it would be like to command the cold, diabetes, cancer, high blood pressure, or whatever sickness is on you, to leave in the name of Jesus Christ, and that spirit obeyed immediately! **Matthew 8:16 Jesus cast out the evil spirits with a simple command, and He healed all the sick.—"He took our sicknesses and removed our diseases."** Jesus also, tells us in **John 14:12 "I tell you the truth, anyone who believes in Me will do the same works I have done, and even greater works, because I am going to be with the Father. You can ask for anything in My name, and I will do it, so that the Son can bring glory to the Father. Yes ask me for anything in my name, and I will do it!"** Is it really that simple or are there other requirements related to God's promises? Keeping in mind, God's love is unconditional but, His promise are conditional. There is nothing we can do to make God love us anymore or less. We can't earn His love, for He chose to love us unconditionally before we were even born. However, most if not all, of His promises are conditional. Let's take a look at some of those promises and conditions so we don't confuse them with His love. Why do we have infirmities, sickness, diseases and what keeps us from a healings? Does God allow sickness to afflict us?

What are the obstacles which can hinder or prevent healing? How can we get victory over infirmities and diseases?

We live in a time of blaming, finger pointing, tongue lashing, lies, and concealing guilt. So, we first need to look inside our own heart, by using Scripture as our gauge, to establish it's condition. This requires absolute honesty. Through this self-analysis investigation, we can learn exactly who we are and how does Christ fit into our lives. Along the way, we build a stronger relationship with our God.

When God created the earth there were no diseases, sickness, infirmities or sin. God made a perfect planet with sinless humans. Diseases, sickness and sin entered the world when Adam and Eve chose to be disobedient to God, therefore, committing the first sin. The penalty for sin is death, as sin causes physical and spiritual death. Ever since the Garden the world has been plagued with deadly diseases and afflictions. The blame game, also started in the Garden of Eden with Eve blaming Satan for her disobediences and sin, and Adam blaming Eve for his part and then blaming God because God gave him Eve in the first place! How's that for blame? See, nothing has changed with our sinful nature since the Garden. People are still blaming others and Satan is still convincing us that his lies are truth.

Satan deceives the world by telling us lies, such as sin is not sin but instead it is an illness and that is not your fault. Who of us wouldn't want to believe that? **John 8:43-46 Jesus said: Why do you not understand what I am saying? It is because you cannot hear My Word. "You are of your father the devil, and you want to do the desires of your father. He was a murderer from the beginning, and does not stand in the truth because there is no truth in him. Whenever he speaks a lie, he speaks from his own nature, for he is a liar and the father of lies. "But because I speak the truth, you do not believe Me. Can any of you prove me guilty of sin? If I am telling the truth, why don't you believe me?"** I would say Jesus makes it very clear that Satan does lie to us and we do act on his lies.

Jesus came to earth to teach God's word and to warn us of the evil one so we will not be deceived. He also paid the price for our sin debt, which is death. Jesus Christ, who was sinless (required by God) shed His own innocent blood to die on a cross for our sins, so that we would have a way back to God when our time on earth had ended. Without this blood sacrifice, which was God's law, no one could return to heaven. **John 3:16 "For God loved the world** so much that He gave His one and only Son, so that everyone who believes in Him will not perish but have eternal life". Did you catch that, **everyone who** believes in Him(conditional). When Jesus took away our sin by His death on the cross He also took away our sickness, diseases and infirmities. **Isaiah 53 . . .** tells us Jesus took our weaknesses and sorrows, and that He was crushed for our sins and pierced for our rebellion. He was beaten so we could be whole; by His stripes (whips) we are healed. So, how is it we are sick and filled with disease? Scriptures actually gives us this answer. We can find answers by the truthfulness of our self-analysis of the heart and soul condition. No one person can do this self-analysis without the help of the Holy Spirit, for we ourselves have a deceptive heart. In other words, we will lie to ourselves and with all sorts of excuses. **Jeremiah 17:9 The heart is deceitful above all things and beyond cure. Who can understand it?** We need to ask God to show us the truth hidden within us. You see, only you and God know the true condition of your heart and spirit. Our lip service doesn't always line up with what is in our secret place of the heart, for no one knows the truth but you and God. Other people only know what we tell them, therefore, others cannot tell us why we are sick or why we have not received the manifestation of a healing. They don't know if God is correcting, doing a work in us, or helping our development along. All they can do is guess. Read, in the bible, the book of Job, and see how much guessing was going on with Job's conditions. It is important that we understand God does not make us sick. He may, however, allow it. We have two sources for our sickness and diseases. Satan and ourselves, and these two are much intertwined. Did you know the majority of diseases and illnesses are sin related or self—inflected? I know, this is the part that is not easy to accept, but its true. Let's look at the sin of gluttony. Gluttony of food produces obesity and obesity may bring forth diabetes, heart disease, high blood pressure, obscene pressure on the skeletal system causing weakening bones and back deformities, bad cholesterol and many, many more ailments that are deadly. How about gluttony of alcohol that can produce liver diseases such as cirrhoses of the liver, diabetes, and a host of other physical diseases, to say nothing of the lives and marriages alcohol destroys. **Proverbs 23:19-22, Listen, my son, and be wise, and keep your heart on the right path. Do not join those who drink too much wine or gorge themselves on meat, for drunkards and gluttons become poor and drowsiness clothes them in**

rags. Do you like honey? Don't eat too much of it, or it will make you sick!

Then, there are the folks who need to take prescription drugs because of their disease they inherited from their own sin. These drugs may cause more damage to the body creating a vicious cycle. Now, let's add a few other insults or offenses to our bodies, such as cigarette smoking, use of recreational drugs, and a lack of exercise which keeps the body from functioning properly. The sin list is absolutely enormous and most people don't realize all these diseases are related to sin, or perhaps they do realize it but it is less convicting when we blame someone or something else for our sickness. We can get all these medical issues from sin and that's before we even touch on mental health problems caused by sins against us. In all of these areas we have given Satan a mighty foothold into our lives.

Jesus in all His mercy has given us a way out. **1 Peter 2:24 (speaking of Jesus) "He personally carried the load of our sins in His body when He died on the cross, so that we can be finished with sin and live a good life from now on. For His wounds have healed ours!" Psalms 103:3 "He forgives all my sins. He heals me" James 5:14,15 "Is anyone sick he should call for the elders of the church and they should pray over him and pour a little oil upon him, calling on the Lord to heal him. And their prayer, if offered in faith, will heal him. For the Lord will make him well: and if his sickness was caused by some sin, the Lord will forgive him."** Not only will the Lord heal us, He will also forgive us for our sins that caused the sickness.

The Holy Bible has certainly established the truth of healings and how sin sickness and disease all fit together. We have been given enough information and wisdom to know God wants us to get a grip on the truth and stop believing Satan and this unbelieving world. Just how reasonable is it, anyway, that we should expect God to heal our bodies, while we continue to sin against it? Sometimes its just difficult to comprehend the thinking of a person who is smoking two packs of cigarettes a day and chooses not to quit, yet gets angry because God, who he does not honor, has not healed him of lung cancer! We are accountable for our own bodies, so we need to ask ourselves what sins are we committing against our body. What about the person who is in pain from morning till night with severe back, hip, and knee problems? Should that person miraculously expect a miracle healing, even though they are 200 pounds plus over weight? Too many people expect God to heal them as they continue in their sin against their body. Preventative medicine is just as important as is correcting the sin against the body. You know the language; eat healthy, plenty of sleep, lots of water, etc. The Bible tells us that our body is the temple of God and we need to treat it with love and respect. **1 Corinthians 3:16 "Don't you realize that all of you together are the house of God, and that the Spirit of God lives among you in His house: If anyone defiles and spoils God's home, God will destroy him. For God's home is holy and clean and you are that home." Romans 12:1 "I plead with you to give your bodies to God. Let them be a living sacrifice, holy, the kind He can accept. Ask the Lord Jesus Christ to help you live as you should, and don't make plans to enjoy evil."**

The state I live in has a law on their books that helps remove guilt from the guilty and give guilt to the non guilty. Let's say a person had visited many bars and had enough alcohol to drink, to meet the definition as legally drunk. The drunk goes into one more bar, for the road, and orders a drink. Now he appears sober, no red flags that would lead one to believe he has had a few drinks already. Now he has two drinks and leaves. However, on his way home he gets into a car accident and it is his fault. Okay so far? Now, in this state, the last bar this person had been drinking in. would be responsible for this person's accident!!! Our society is every so slowly moving away from punishing the guilty. Drug addicts that overdose and die, the family can blame and sue the supplier, if they can find one, even if it is a doctor or doctors. No responsibility to the dead addict, the money is in the supplier. It does not matter if the addict had been seeing many different doctors and the doctors didn't know about each other! A political figure was shot, and one political party blamed the other political party even though neither political party had anything to do with it. We are excusing people by not making them accountable for their own wrongdoing. All of this blaming is sure giving Satan a happy day. Individuals need to get well so our society can heal, and we can't get healed until we get honest.

Having worked in the medical field for 40 plus years, I can tell you the shocking truth, that many, many people do not want to be healed or to be well! Sad isn't it? Oh sure, there are many different reasons for this deficiency, and some of the patients are aware of this state of mental health, but most are not. Some people are just so needy for love and attention that they would stop at nothing to get their needs met. They truly believe the only way to get their emptiness filled is with their body. Some of them use treacherous relationships and others use sickness, either genuine or counterfeit. God, of course has a better way. **Philippians 4:19 "God who takes care of me will supply all your needs from His glorious riches, which have been given to us in Christ Jesus." 1Timothy 5:3 The church should care for any widow who has no one else to care for her."** Yes it is true, we will reap what we sow. So what is it that you need? **Galatians 6:7 Don't be misled. Remember that you can't ignore God and get away with it. You will always reap what you sow!"**

I remember this one patient, when she was a little girl, in her mind, she could only get the love and attention she needed from her parents if she were injured or sick. It didn't take her long to realize she could use sickness to get her emotional needs met. When she needed reassurance that she was loved she would be sick. Consequently, she spent her entire life using this method for love and attention. She lived, or should I say existed for seventy two years always being sick and depressed. She died never realizing that Jesus could and would have met all her needs, and that it was not necessary for her to live out her life being miserable and unhappy.

Unfortunately, her story is all too familiar for many hurting folks and it need not be that way. Always being sick and depressed is truly a miserable existence, and it is not the Will of God. Depression and sickness are spirits coming against us, and Jesus has told us to rebuke these spirits. The "poor me" syndrome only makes one physically and emotionally sicker and never brings about a favorable outcome for anyone. If anything, people tend to stay away from individuals that harbor these unwanted spirits, because they are contagious. Physicians often refer to these patients as hypochondriac. (person who worries or talks excessively about his or her health: an individual preoccupied with their health or disease and are so intense that it disrupts normal living habits)

Refusing to accept an illness does not mean we are denying what is attacking our body. We cannot just sit back and accept Satan's attacks. **James 4:7 "So give yourselves humbly to God, resist the devil and he will flee from you." Matthew 8:7 10:1-8 Yes Jesus said, "I will come and heal him. He gave authority to cast out evil spirits and to heal every kind of sickness and disease. Heal the sick, raise the dead, cure the lepers, and cast out demons."** Why is it so difficult to believe what Jesus tells us?

Our lack of faith will keep us in bondage and give Satan the foothold in us that he desires. Instead we need to believe and act on the Word of God.

When we say or hear others say, "my sore throat, my high blood pressure, my cancer, my diabetes, my depression, my ulcer, my cold or any other disease, we are saying or hearing acceptance of these ills. Sometimes, this ownership is said with much pride and delight and sometimes it's said with a sorrowful look or a poor me voice, that only validates Satan and his work on you. Denying to take ownership of disease and illness is different than not accepting. Denying would be to ignore the symptom or evidence of said illness or disease. However, non accepting is to fight the symptoms of the illness or disease with the power of Jesus Christ and know with certainty, without doubt that we are healed before the symptoms are even gone. God's Word contains healing power! **Proverbs 3:7-8 Do not be wise in your own eyes; fear the Lord and shun evil. This will bring health to your body and nourishment to your bones."** This all means that: We must live in a humble and dutiful subjection to God and His government: fear the Lord, as your Sovereign Lord and Master; be ruled in everything by your religion and subject to the Divine will. This must be, a humble subjection; be not wise in your own eyes. There is not a greater enemy to the power of religion, and the fear of God in the heart, than conceitedness of our own wisdom. Those that have an opinion of their own sufficiency think it below them, and a disparagement to them, to take their measures from, much more to hamper themselves with, religion's rules. This must also be a dutiful subjection: fear the Lord, and depart from evil; take heed of doing anything to offend Him and forfeit His care. To fear the Lord, so as to depart from evil, is true wisdom and understanding; those that have it are truly wise, but self-denyingly so, and not wise in their own eyes. For our encouragement thus to live in the fear of God it is here promised that it shall be as serviceable even to the outward man as our necessary food. It will be nourishing: it shall be health to thy navel. It will be strengthening: it shall be marrow to thy bones. The prudence, temperance, and sobriety, the calmness and composure of mind, and the good government of the appetites and passions, which religion teaches, tend very much not only to the health of the soul, but to a good habit of body, which is very desirable, and without which our other enjoyments in this world are insipid. Envy is the rottenness of the bones; the sorrow of the world dries them; but hope and joy in God are marrow to them. (from Commentary Matthew Henry).

I know this is not easy to do, as it goes against our very own nature, but remember our nature is sinful and evil. Sinful means to do "what the flesh wants." That's why Jesus sent us His Holy Spirit to take off our old sinful nature and put on our righteous nature by committing to and following Jesus Christ, also know as being born again.

God does not want us sick, but Satan does. Remember he is the destroyer. Satan will have as much power over our bodies as we allow him to have, so don't give him power by falling into his traps. If we suddenly discovered we have a sore throat, we should treat the symptoms for comfort and rebuke the sickness. Out loud (as Satan cannot read our minds, he can only plant thoughts), command the spirits of sickness to leave our body immediately, in the name of Jesus Christ. Don't speak of it to anyone, for saying "I have a sore throat" is taking ownership and giving a foothold and power to Satan. Instead, thank Jesus for your healing and move on. Be strong in faith and believe God's Word. If you waiver in faith ask God to help you with your unbelief. Be honest with Him, tell Him you are having a problem believing and our faithful God will help you to believe.

Spiritually, we are all in different places at different times, however, the responsibilities are the same. Each of us must be accountable for God's temple (our own body) to be well cared for. Whether we go to the church elders for laying on of hands, holy oil and prayer, or see a medical doctor or a naturopath, it makes no difference in the method of healing just as long as it is by God's direction. God will let you know what path of action is necessary in alignment with your spiritual walk, so ask God. The Book of James says you have not because you ask not. In other words, we need to let God use whatever method He chooses for our healing, as we know God heals in many ways.

Our God is a healing God, and He desires for His children to be healthy and happy. We don't want to see our children suffer from diseases and sickness, and our Heavenly Father doesn't want His children to suffer either. Yet, so many people are willing to accept inflections on their bodies, because they consciously or subconsciously believe they deserve the affliction. For a variety of reasons people feel unworthy of God's blessings of good health and they deserve to be sick because of past sins. We don't deserve

God's blessing, and if we got what we do deserved we would all be sentenced to death and hell. That is exactly why Jesus died for us so we wouldn't get what we deserve. Jesus saved us from sin's hold and death's grip on us. **Titus 3:4-5 "God our Savior showed us His kindness and love. He saved us, not because of the good things we did but because of His mercy. He washed away our sins and gave us a new life through the Holy Spirit."**

Now what about the very young child that dies of an illness or disease? Even though we parents have the responsibility to stand in the gap for our very young children, exercise our faith, and stand on the promises of God, we must also remember God has the final say. We may not always know or understand why God chooses a direction, far different than what we hoped for, but we do know His decision is always the right decision. **Isaiah 55:8-9 "For My thoughts are not your thoughts, neither are your ways My ways," declares the Lord. "As the heavens are higher than the earth, so are My ways higher than your ways and My thoughts than your thoughts."** Children belong to God and we parents are their caretakers only until God chooses to take them home. Through our prayers and faith God will heal the child, if it is His Will to do so. If it is not His Will, He will take the child home to Himself. This, of course, is true of all of us. We all have an appointed time that we will leave this earth. **Hebrews 9:27 And inasmuch as it is appointed for men to die once and after this comes judgment" Psalm 116:15 Precious in the sight of the Lord is the death of His godly ones."**

Sometimes our human selfish nature gets in the way of us accepting God's plan. I know parents who begged God not to take their sick child even if it meant that the child would not have a good quality life and he would suffer immeasurably. Our love for our children can be so intense that we lose sight of our child's need and desires. Yes, it is extremely difficult and painful to let go of someone we love so desperately, especially if it is a young child. For whatever reason his life was cut short, we can take comfort knowing all very young children are accepted back to God. We don't always understand God's timing, but our life belongs to God and we do have the duty to be obedient in what God has purposed for our life. God decides how He will use our lives, and our obedience will be rewarded and when our purpose has been fulfilled; He will take us home, also.

About eight years ago our church's Senior Pastor was very ill. He had been battling leukemia for many years with all the traditional treatment such as chemotherapy and blood transfusions and such. He lead a congregation of twelve thousand plus and was very much loved throughout the world. All of us were praying for a miracle, a miraculous healing, but that was not to be for God had other plans. Pastor Ron Mehl was the most humble, spiritual and Christ like man I have ever known. He continued, throughout his illness, to give glory to God and to feed his flock with the truth of God's Word; he humbly shepherded with godly wisdom and integrity. Ron didn't focus on his imminent death, instead he always kept his focus on the now, for there is no promise of tomorrow. **James 4:14 "How do you know what will happen tomorrow? For your life is like the morning fog . . . it's here a little while, then it's gone."**

All, who knew him, were well aware that God used Ron's illness to help so many others suffering from fear, sickness and diseases. He brought so much encouragement to the very sick, to the wayward child, to the lost soul and to this very world, crippled with evil. He showed us how to live and how to die. May 30, 2003, God took Ron Mehl home to be with Him, and He gave Ron a new body without disease. We know God did answer our prayers because Ron now lives disease free and pain free and in the comfort of our Heavenly Father's home!

If you are in need of a healing, first do everything humanly possible such as change lifestyle, lose weight, eat healthy, exercise, stop smoking, drugs, drinking and do, whatever is necessary, to be healthy and God will step in when you can't do anymore. Pray and ask God what His plan is for you. Go to Scriptures and write every Scripture that has to do with healing and pray them back to the Lord. Exercise your faith muscle and stand on every promise in God's Word, regardless of how long it takes and give glory and thanks to God for what He is about to do. **Hebrews 11:1-2 "What is faith? It is the confident assurance that something we want is going to happen. It is the certainty that what we hope for is waiting for us. Even though we cannot see it up ahead. Men of God in days of old were famous for their faith!" Matthew 8:17 "He took our sicknesses and bore our diseases."**

It is important to know God's Will, as how can you stand on a promise you don't know or believe. Fear is not a spirit from God. It is Satan that dishes up fear and disbelief in us. Don't assume everything that happens in this life is God's Will. God wants everyone to be saved, but they won't be. God wants every soul to be back with Him, but they won't be. God wants everyone to follow His Son Jesus Christ, but they won't. Remember, God gave man a free will to choose who they will follow. If we don't follow our Lord and His teachings why would we expect to have a healing from the very one we resist, defy and rebel against?

Jesus gave us wonderful promises of healings, so rebuke the evil spirits and take hold of what our Lord says. **"Jesus Christ is the same yesterday, today and forever." Hebrews 13:8,** Rely on His truth and rebuke the lies of Satan. God is faithful and He has a wonderful plan for your live. Trust in Him and keep on trusting. Your healing may not come when and how you think it should, but it will come, and just at the right time. **Habakkuk 2:3 "If it seems slow, do not despair, for these things will surely come to pass. Just be patient! They will not be over due a single day!"**

Believe the Master Planner of your life, believe God's truth. **Mark 11:22-24 Jesus said "Have faith in God." "Truly I say to you, whoever says to this mountain, Be taken up and cast into the sea, and does not doubt in his heart, but believes that what he says is going to happen, it will be granted him." "Therefore I say to you, all things, for which you pray and ask, believe that you have received them, and they will be granted you." "But when you are praying, first forgive anyone you are holding a grudge against, so that your Father in heaven will forgive your sins, too."**

God of Abraham, Isaac, and Jacob, our God Creator of heaven and earth, determines the length of time we have on this earth, right down to the year, day, minute, and second. We however, given a *free will*, will determine the quality of life and how we use it. If our choice of *quality* prohibits us from accomplishing the works God has purposed for us, we will be held accountable to Him. This is why we have healing promises throughout Scripture, and it is up to us to take hold and use our faith muscle. **Ephesians 5:6 Let no one deceive you with empty arguments, for God's wrath is coming on the disobedient.**

Love your body and treat it well, so it may serve our Lord and you in its fullness. The way we treat our bodies is a reflection of our love for our Lord Jesus Christ.

Jesus had some words for us regarding love. **Matthew 22:37-40 Jesus said: "Love the Lord your God with all your** heart and with all your soul and with all your mind." "This is the first and greatest commandment. And the second is like it: Love your neighbor as yourself." All other commandments and all the demands of the prophets are based on these two commandments."

CHAPTER TWELVE

John 8:32 "And you will know the truth, and the truth will set you free." **Romans 8:2** "Because you belong to Him. The power of the life-giving Spirit has freed you."

DELIVERANCE FROM ADDICTION

Let's face it, we are creatures of habit and that is just one of the characteristics of the human species. You might say, that's the way we're wired; also, most of us, do have an addictive personality. We have compulsive behaviors and we often act on our irresistible impulses regardless of our rationality skills. **Proverbs 23:2 & 20-21 And put a knife to your throat if you are a man given to appetite (food, alcohol, sex, etc) Do not associate with winebibbers; be not among them nor among gluttonous eaters of meat, (Isaiah 5:22; Luke 21:34; Romans 13:13; Eph 5:18) For the drunkard and the glutton shall come to poverty, and drowsiness shall clothe a man with rags.** In other words, we all have addictive traits. Some of our compulsions could be with food abuse, anorexia, prescription or recreational drugs, sex, gambling, cigarette smoking, pornography, cigar/ pipe smoking, foul language, alcohol, work, play, exercising, people pleasing and a host of other scenarios. All of us have something that controls a piece of our lives even when we try to overcome the urges. While much of our compulsions are brought about from our own insecurities and the need for control, we must not forget that the enemy of God is always diligently at work, helping us to forget that anything we do that brings harm to our body, mind, soul, or to others, and does not bring glory to God is a sin, regardless of our own excuses or personal beliefs.

The secular society takes the position that addiction is a sickness or a disease, therefore, eliminating blame or responsibility for the addict. There is no biblical premise for this, however, the contrary is found throughout scripture, and man is held responsible for asking God to help them overcome. **I Corinthians 6:19-20 Do you not know that your body is the temple (the very sanctuary) of the Holy Spirit who lives within you, Whom you have received as a gift from God? You are not your own, you were bought with a price (purchased with a preciousness and paid for, made His own). So then, honor God and bring glory to Him in your body. Romans 8:13 For if you live according to (the dictates of) the flesh, you will surely die. But if through the power of the Holy Spirit you are habitually putting to death (Making extinct, deadening) the evil deeds prompted by the body, you shall (really and genuinely) live forever.** Where there is no guilt or remorse there will be no change or repentance. Guilt is necessary to lead us to the knowledge of sin which then brings us to repentance toward God. **Romans 3:20 For no person will be justified (made righteous, acquitted, and judged acceptable) in His sight by observing the works prescribed by the law (which brings knowledge of sin). For the real function of the law is to make men recognize and be conscious of sin (not mere perception, but an acquaintance with sin which works towards repentance, faith, and holy character). James 2:10 For whosoever keeps the law as a whole but stumbles and offends in one single instance has become guilty of breaking all of it.** God gave us a conscience, and from this we have guilt to guide us in knowing right from wrong. Over time, sin will deaden our conscience. **I Timothy 4:1-2 God's Spirit specifically tells us that in latter days there will be men who abandon the true faith and allow themselves to be spiritually seduced by teachings of demons, teachings given by men who are lying hypocrites, whose consciences are as dead as seared flesh. JB Phillips** Society believes there are no absolutes, but God's word teaches us just the opposite, and we must choose either the worlds view or God's. We, alone, get ourselves into bondage and we must take responsibility for our own decision. **Galatians 5:1 In this freedom Christ has made us free and completely liberated us; stand fast then, and do not be entangled again with the yoke of bondage.** One thing I know for sure is that we have a merciful God who would be more than willing to free us. All we need to do is ask. God may choose to deliver someone immediately from their bondage, or he may choose to set them free over time. For everything God chooses to do will be for the good of our development and to teach us lessons that will make us mentally and spiritually strong, and to build our faith and trust in Him, only. Did God put these curses of addiction on us? No He did not. Would you put a curse on your child that you love with all your heart? However, we do hold on to our family culture and learned behavior. Also, our family values, traditions, traits, and weaknesses do contribute to our addictions, simply by our upbringing, training, exposures and our childhood experiences. It is not unusual for a child, of an alcoholic, to swear when he/she grows up they will never be like their alcoholic parent. When the child gets older he justifies taking an alcohol drink by telling himself, *I will only have one drink, it's been a tough day*," hum, wonder where he heard that excuse. Before he knows it he is a carbon copy of the alcoholic parent. By focusing on the alcoholic parent he became an alcoholic. God also says the sins of the Father are passed to the Children. God's word says each child must choose to follow in their father's steps or to follow God. By not choosing God, you automatically choose to follow the father. This is how alcoholism gets passed on no matter the resolve of the child. Alcoholism is not a disease it IS a sin. That's why the bible warns us about the danger of drinking alcohol. A drink is not a sin, Jesus did share wine and He made wine for a wedding, it's the drinks that follow that become the sin. We are far better off refusing any activity or substance that we know is a weakness for us or known to be a family weakness. We need not give Satan permission or a foothold over our lives by giving him an open door. **I Peter 5:8 Be well balanced (temperate, sober of mind), be vigilant and cautious at all times; for that enemy of yours, the devil, roams around like a lion roaring in fierce hunger, seeking someone to seize upon and devour. Amplified**

It is truly unfortunate for the person that God delivers from their addiction and they quickly forget who gave them their gift of freedom. **Deuteronomy 4:9 Only take heed, and guard your life diligently, lest you forget the things which your eyes have seen and lest they depart from your mind and heart all the days of your life.** If one does not give God the glory and thanks daily, they put themselves in jeopardy of relapsing because of a prideful attitude. A puffed-up behavior will ultimately be the source of their relapse. **I Corinthians 10:12 Therefore let anyone who thinks he stands (who feels sure that he has a steadfast mind**

and is standing firm), take heed lest he fall into sin. When we remember God's favor and mercy and give Him thanks, it will keep us humble and safe before our Lord.

Over seventeen years ago I used to smoke, and I must admit I did truly enjoy smoking and never had any intention on quitting. Of coarse, I convinced myself that I was not harming anyone and this was not a sin. After all, if I were to admit it was wrong I would then be deliberately sinning and would have to do something about it, like STOP. The thinking of an addict! I went so far, that I convinced myself that I could tell others about the love of Christ and they would not think anything wrong with me having a cigarette. I am not sure how I thought I could justify smoking, when the Bible makes it clear we need to treat our bodies as a holy temple and bring glory to God, and smoking did just the opposite. When we surrender our lives to Jesus Christ, our body then belongs to Him and we must treat it with respect and excellence. I think maybe I just skipped over that part so I need not change or repent. Talk about lying to oneself! Oh, but God had a different plan for me.

One morning I was getting ready for work, I worked in a hospital, and I sat down at my makeup table with my coffee and cigarettes. As I prepared to light my cigarette I had an overwhelming sense of **no, don't.** Not knowing what that was all about, I hurried and got ready for work. When I got in my car I went to light up a cigarette, and again had that same overwhelming feeling of **no.** So, I waited until I got to work and on my break I went to have a cigarette, yep, you guessed it, it happened again. Only this time I was suspicious of this being the Lord. Of course I tried several more times during the day to have a cigarette with the same results. By the end of the day I went to the hospital chapel to have a little discussion with the Lord of why I should be able to smoke.

During this time I never had the fear or thought that God would strike me down with lightning, or kill me or some other harmful fate. I did, however, have the feeling that if I disobeyed and smoked, that God would withhold blessings. I sort of remember going back to the chapel at a later date, and asked God what those blessings might be, that I would miss out on. In my addict mind, I wanted to weigh out the blessing versus the cigarettes, wow, what was I thinking!

The doctors in the emergency room, where I worked, were very supportive, but I don't think they understood me when I told them, not smoking was not my idea, and I was not a happy camper with my situation. The truth being known, I would have smoked in a heartbeat, if only I knew what those blessings were. It was the fear of not being blessed that kept me from lighting a cigarette, or so I thought.

Over the next few weeks I felt like a volcano ready to explode with the pressure of frustration and anxiety building. I remember, there was a woman walking by the hospital with a cigarette in her hand and I wanted to run outside and take it away from her. Not because I felt it was harmful for her, it was more like me wanting it for myself. My frustration and anxiety became apparent to me, when I would get home from work the children would leave and the dog would hide; I knew I had a problem! Several more days had passed when I finally reached my breaking point. I was at work and it was my break time so I went up to the chapel to inform the Lord, I was done. I cried, and I prayed, but nothing happened. So, I got up and told the Lord I was going downstairs to have a cigarette; I could not do this any longer. When I got downstairs, the emergency room was so busy it appeared as though every ambulance in the city came in at one time. Needless to say, I had to get back to work instead of having a cigarette. When my shift was over I went home without giving cigarettes a thought. It was not until the next day when I was at work that I realized the frustration and anxiety had been removed! It's not the desire for a cigarette that makes us smoke its the anxiety level and the frustration that brings us back to smoking. It is by the Grace of God and His faithfulness that I remain smoke-free today.

I have listened to many patients tell me that they would give anything in the world to stop smoking. The more I hear their stories the more I realize what rich blessings I have received when God took my cigarette away. Unbeknownst to me, my children had been praying for the Lord to make me stop smoking. I am so grateful that Jesus Christ honored the prayers of my children and he worked in me until he had me in a place of obedience. It is still hard to believe I actually thought I could witness for the Lord while sinning against my own body. I have come to the conclusion that addictions are not only sinful but they make us think stupid! **Jesus said "if you hold on to my teachings—you will know the truth and the truth will set you free" John 8:32-32**

God does not want us to live in bondage, the enemy does. What God wants for us, is the life that he has planned for. On the other hand, Satan would love to keep us tied up in bondage until the sin kills us. The lie that we suffer from a disease instead of sin, is the very lie Satan wants us to believe so we will not feel guilty and repent or rely on God to set us free. The enemy (Satan) will continue to put every excuse imaginable in our mind that will keep us tied to the lie. Only God can free us, but we must call on Him. In my case, my children called on Jesus to set their mother free from cigarettes. **Jesus says in <u>Matthew 7:7,8</u> "Ask, and you will be given what you ask for. Seek, and you will find. Knock, and the door will be opened. For everyone who asks, receives. Anyone who seeks, finds. If only you will knock, the door will open"**

Don't be afraid to stand on the promises of God. Just remember it is God who wants us free to choose a peaceful, righteous, loving and exciting life with Him, so we can be sure He <u>will</u> fulfill His promises when we purpose to believe Him. Call on God to protect you from the evil one. Remember that you can pray to Our Heavenly Father in the name of Jesus Christ, and your Father will hear your prayer. **<u>1 Corinthians 6:12</u> "I can do anything I want to if Christ has not said no, but some of these things aren't good for me. Even if I am allowed to do them, I'll refuse to if I think they might get such a grip on me that I can't easily stop when I want to." <u>Ephesians 6:10</u> "Last of all I want to remind you that your strength must come from the Lord's mighty power within you."**

I know the power that addiction can hold over us. I also know that I would be smoking today if it were not for the faithfulness, mercy and love, and power of Jesus Christ at work in me. God took away my cigarettes out of love, not using condemnation, but using love and one authoritative word, **no!** Deep in my being, I knew every **no** I heard was from God.

God also loves you, and will set you free from your addiction(s). All you need to do is ask, trust, and obey Him. God is not limited. He will show you the way out of your bondage. He has the power over the enemy; that's why, when we rebuke the devil in the name of Jesus, he must flee. Its Jesus' authority that he must obey. **<u>James 4:7</u> So humble yourselves before God. Resist the devil and he will flee from you".** Don't be afraid to surrender your all to your Heavenly Father, after all He is on your side. Go with His plan for your life, and achieve the <u>daily</u> success He desires for you. Remember to live in the now, not tomorrow or yesterday, and just go with each day, one day at a time.

CHAPTER THIRTEEN

Matthew 6:14-15 "For if you forgive men when they sin against you, your heavenly Father will also forgive you. But if you do not forgive men of their sins, your Father will not forgive your sins.

FORGIVNESS

Forgiveness is not only a huge part of our spiritual growth, but it's a necessity for our soul to survive. Harboring offenses will web an infectious cancer throughout our soul, mind and body. A unforgiving heart layered with resentment is a recipe for mental imprisonment or even death. The unforgiving spirit will open the door for Satan to accomplish his purpose, to destroy one's body and soul.

This unforgiving spirit will cause the body to suffer, acutely, with depression, anger, eating disorders, stress, anxiety neurosis, fear, meanness, selfish behavior, bad temper; all of this leads to high blood pressure, heart disease and cancer, just to name a few illnesses caused by a unforgiving spirit. Satan will camouflage un-forgiveness to look like sickness, so one will treat the symptoms instead of dealing with the root. Satan will always want the opposite of God. God wants you well, happy, and whole; only He can restore what Satan has damaged. God can and will reestablish, rebuild, replace, reshape, and repair your body, mind and soul, but it all starts with you . . . . FORGIVINESS! **Ephesians 4:26—31"And don't sin by letting anger gain control over you. Don't let the sun go down while you are still angry, for anger gives a mighty foothold to the Devil. Stop being mean, bad tempered and angry. Instead, be kind to each other, tenderhearted, forgiving one another, just as God has forgiven you."**

We often associate forgiveness with excusing ones bad or even evil behavior. We think if we forgive, we are excusing or condoning the actions and behavior of the perpetrator. We are NOT! We are freeing ourselves from the chains of Satan. The perpetrator is still guilty and will still be accountable to God. Rid yourself of any and all fantasy paybacks, and leave the justice to God. When your perpetrator gets his deserved punishment, do not rejoice in his penalty inflicted, or treatment. **Proverbs 20:22 Don't repay evil for evil. Wait for the Lord to handle the matter. 24:29 Don't say," Now I can pay him back for all his meanness to me!" Romans 12:19-20 Beloved, never avenge yourselves, but leave the way open for God's wrath; for it is written, Vengeance is Mine, I well repay, says the Lord. But if your enemy is hungry, feed him; if he is thirsty, give him drink; for by so doing you will heap burning coals upon his head.**

We live in an evil, fallen world where many hideous, horrific, and outrageous things happen to good people and young children. This world is Satan's domain; It's his territory and we are all subject to his evil works. All this evilness is the fallout of the disobedience in the Garden of Eden, but it does not mean we need to fall prey. As difficult as it may be, do NOT allow Satan to gain control of you because your heart doesn't want to forgive. Ask God to forgive your unforgiving heart and pray to Him to give you a forgiving heart and ask Him to show you how to do this. I do know this, if you do not forgive, but indulge in this all consuming emotion of bitterness and hate, it will cause your heart to be hardened and cold, and this will destroy you.

Some of the people we need to forgive are now dead, but you can still forgive them. Those whom you can't, or choose not to see in person can still be forgiven. Close your eyes and imagine they are in the room with you. Tell that person what they did to you and how they hurt you and tell them you forgive them. This may sound easy but I can tell you, from experience, it is not. It took me many tries and a lot of praying before I could do this, from my heart and mean it. Only with God's help, was I able to truly forgive my abusive perpetrator. Pray for God to ready your heart.

There is another person whom we find it very, very difficult to forgive, and that is self! So many people repent to God and ask Him to forgive them, but they won't forgive themselves. Jesus tells us to forgive those who sinned against us and that includes we who sinned against ourselves. If we don't love and forgive ourselves, we have no heart to love and forgive others. Don't sabotage yourself and your future with self-hatred and self-loathing. Some people have so much self-hate that they punish themselves with dishonor and disgrace all because they truly despise themselves and feel unworthy of love and forgiveness. Repent to God and ask for forgiveness from those you have wronged including yourself. Don't hang onto the garbage of the past, rid yourself of that unforgiving demonic spirit; God will make you new. To hang on to past grievances, resentments, imaginary paybacks, and hate will destroy you. You must forgive in order to be free, so you can move forward in God's plan for your life. If you choose not to forgive, your growth will be stunted and you will remain frozen in time.

Forgiveness does not take away the sins of the perpetrator or wrongdoer, only our Lord has that power. Forgiveness frees the victim from the terror and fear of the past. Consequences from the choices that have been made will still play out regardless. The prisons are full of people who are truly sorry and have repented, however, they will remain in prison until their punishment has been accomplished. Regrettably, many victims are forced to live with physical consequences of their perpetrator's actions, but know this, what Satan has meant for evil God will turn it around and use it for your good. To forgive or not to forgive, to sin or not to sin, are all choices we have, so make the choice that sets you free from Satan and ties you to your Heavenly Father, God Almighty. **Romans 8:28 And we know that God causes everything to work together for the good of those who love God and are called according to His purpose for them."** Don't try to even the score as revenge belongs to the Lord. **Leviticus 19:17-18 "Do not nurse hatred in your heart"** ... **"Never seek revenge or bear a grudge against anyone ... I am the Lord."**

CHAPTER FOURTEEN

2Corinthians 6:14 "Don't team up with those who are unbelievers. How can righteousness be a partner with wickedness? How can light live with darkness?"

FIND YOUR RIGHT MATE

We live in a society that has become restless and insecure in our relationships, vocations and with life in general. Our world seems to be lacking so much, in the moral and accountability category, to say nothing of the love and trust department. Things are, dangerously out of control in our new world. So much so, we have become overly skeptical and suspicious, making it, almost, impossible to trust anyone with our hearts, emotions and secrets, and all those other things that real friends share.

Relationships of today are short lived, mostly, because they lack commitment and honesty. Today, many marriages are good only until things get difficult. Employer and employee, only good until something better comes along. Friends are good until disagreements. All good relationships need to have good solid attributes such as trust, commitment, honesty, communication and godly characteristic, that spell success. Instead, we seem to lack in all of these things, giving good relationships a zero value. When relationships end, regardless of their duration, many people are left feeling insecure, disillusioned and some just get lost in the wake of the storm, such as the children.

God established the foundation of marriage and family. If we truly want a forever marriage and a strong happy family, we will need to play by God's rules not ours. All relationships, not just marriage, should be entered into with the blessing and like minded of God. In other words, make sure, what you are about to do is the *will* of God and lines up with the Word of God.

What is God's *will* for your life. Is marriage part of God's plan for you. Do you know God's desires for your future? Do you know your true desire for your future? The Bible speaks a lot about marriage and divorce and what is sin and what is not sin. Should you marry or not and what about divorce. The book of **Matthew chapter 19:3-12 Jesus said 19:8 "Moses permitted divorce only as a concession to your hard hearts, but it was not what God had originally intended. I tell you this, whoever divorces his wife and marries someone else commits adultery-unless his wife has been unfaithful. Some choose not to marry for the sake of the Kingdom of Heaven. Let anyone accept this who can. A man leaves his father and mother and is joined to his wife, and the two are united into one."** Gives us a clear picture what is expected of us. Paul addresses marriage questions in **1 Corinthians 7:1-39 7:8,9 "So I say to those who aren't married and to widows—it's better to stay unmarried, just as I am. (the Apostle Paul speaking) But if they can't control themselves, they should go ahead and marry. It's better to marry than to burn with lust." 7:3 "Yes, it is good to abstain from sexual relations. But because there is so much sexual immorality, each man should have his own wife, and each woman should have her own husband".** Both books, Matthew and 1 Corinthians, are very helpful in guiding us through the many questions whether marriage is right for you, as an individual, and what God expects.

If you come to the conclusion that it is your desire to be married, try this exercise. Sit down with pen and paper and make a realistic list of the type of person you want as, a marriage partner, and all the qualities and characteristics you want in this person. Be sure to list religious beliefs, political party, hobbies, type of friends, humor, employment, do they want children, well the list could be very long but it's important. Than make a list of same with your characteristics and what qualities you will bring to the table and on your list, put why you want to marry and how does God fit into your list. Now go over your list with this in mind, **2 Corinthians 6:14 "Do not be yoked together with unbelievers. For what do righteousness and wickedness have in common? Or what fellowship can light have with darkness?"** In the book of **Matthew 19:5 "—and the two will become on flesh"** now bring your list before the Lord with an open mind, for God may change your list, as well as many desires within you.

Marriage is a commitment to God, <u>first.</u> Your body and life belongs to Him. Your needs and desires can only be met by God, who knows your deepest thoughts and desires. God knows more of what you need and want than you do. God never intended for married partners to take over His role, as our supplier. **<u>Philippians 4:19</u> "My God shall supply ALL your needs from His riches in glory, because of what Christ Jesus has done for us."** It is unrealistic and unfair to expect your mate to be responsible for making you happy and fulfilling all your needs, this is God's area and one should not, ever, entertain the idea of marriage, until you have, first, build a lasting, strong, trusting and committed relationship with our Lord God.

When you edify, respect, support, love and trust each other, you and your mate will reap great blessings throughout your marriage. Exalt, encourage, honor and direct your focus on your partner and God will focus on you with His power, character and peace. We always, get back what we give! One should never try to change their mate, for if you pray for God to change your mate, He will first change you.

If God has put the desire in your heart to marry, than you need to put your trust in Him to bring that desire to fulfillment. Partners for life is a gift from God to be cherished. Once again, only God knows the heart and motives of each of us. Let God be your match maker for He is better than any computer, dating service or persons and He will always give you His best. You will never need to settle for second best, so wait on God and go for the Gold!

When you wait on God to bring His choice for you, you can rest assured He has taken in every single consideration for you to have a beautiful relationship filled with God's blessings to give you the marriage He intended for you. When it is the Will of God for you to be married, the desire in you will grow not lessen with time. In His perfect timetable He will have you meet your mate and the Lord will see to it that you know, without a doubt, this person is right for you.

Waiting, is a period of time God will use to get you and your mate ready for each other. If you want God to bring the right person, you will want to obey the commands He has for you to follow. Even if you have broken His commands in the past, its not too late to start over. Ask God for His forgiveness and repent in the name of

Jesus Christ and start from that point, God is a forgiving God. If you choose not to follow His commands, well, lets just say, you're pretty much on your own. You see, God takes the marriage contract very seriously, and the preparation is part of that contract.

The cultures of today have disregarded God's holiness, values and instructions and our society reflects this rebellious behavior with the many, many divorces and immoral life styles, God didn't change nor did He change His mind on what is right in His sight. Society is changing and we are getting it wrong, according to God! So, if we want God's best we need to stick to His plan, regardless of what the world thinks.

God wants us to live pure and holy lives. He commands us to stay out of sexual sin so we can marry in holiness and God shall honor and find favor over our marriages. Pre-material sex is a sin in God's eyes and should be in ours. We need to keep our body and mind pure for our own sake as well as for the mate God brings to us. Satan will use anything, we allow, to get a foothold over us. God will give you the strength over the temptations that Satan will put in front of you. We should not put ourselves or allow others to put us in situations that would compromise our integrity and that Satan could use against us. Many good people fall into Satan's traps by ignoring good old common sense. Do not put yourself in a compromising situation and don't give room for gossip. Each of us have the responsibility to keep ourselves pure and holy before God and the Holy Spirit is always present to help us, for God knows how difficult this can be. **Thessalonians 4:3,4 "For God wants you to be holy and pure, and to keep clear of all sexual sin so that each of you will marry in holiness and honor, no in lustful passion as the heathen do, in their ignorance of God and His ways."**

God "_blessed marriages,_" are not without trials and challenges, all marriages have seasons of trouble. The difference is God seeking, marriages, have God's wisdom, direction and protection. So even though tough times will come, they won't devastate a God-faith marriage. It's your faith that will strengthen the marriage during these trials. The real nightmare would be, not to have God in your decision making and marry the wrong person, and this happens all too often when we are left to our own devises and choices. Having the wrong mate is very costly in terms of heartache, emotions, values, spirituality and finances, to say nothing of children lost in the wake of a divorce storm. If you are following God's rules, divorce should never be an option. Something to that old saying, "those who pray together stay together", remember, love and commitment are choices, not emotions.

Everything God tells us to do, is for our own protection, therefore, God has a particular order He wants us to follow. Above all we must keep God at the very center of our marriage, He must be the anchor, for success. He is the substance that holds a marriage together and God's order must never change, GOD is first, family second and vocation third. God made man first and then he created woman to be man's partner and helper. God never said that one was more important than the other or more valued, as God gave both, men and women, different duties and responsibilities that would please Him. God intended for man to be the head of the family and make the best choices for his family, with God leading man. Men will be accountable to God for the decisions they make. The godly and wise man will seek God's plan as opposed to using his own strategy. The woman is accountable to the man who is the head of the family. This order brings peace and stability strength to the family unit. This does not mean women should have no thoughts or desires of their own. The husband and wife should be of one accord and discuss issues reasonably and fairly leaving the final decision for the man to see to it that God's **Will** is being done and he will be accountable to God for the decision he makes. This is a huge responsibility! See why it is so important to marry a godly mate, can you imagine living in this kind of environment with a nonbeliever! In **Colossians 3:18** Paul gives us, **"Wives, submit to your husbands, as is fitting in the Lord. Husbands, love your wives and do not be harsh with them"**. **Romans 13:10** **"Love does no wrong to anyone. That's why it fully satisfies all God's requirements. It is the only law you need."**

Do you see the importance of allowing God to choose our mates for us? The Bible says husbands and wives are partners in receiving God's blessings, therefore, we are partners in not receiving God's blessings should we as, man and wife disregard God's marriage instructions. **1 Peter 3:7** **"Remember that you and your wife are partners in receiving God's blessing and if you don't treat her as you should your prayers will not get ready answers."**

CHAPTER FIFTEEN

Malachi3:10 "Bring all the tithes into the storehouse so there will be enough food in My Temple. If you do, says the Lord of Heaven, I will open the windows of heaven for you. I will pour out a blessing so great you won't have enough room to take it in! Put me to the test!"

FINANCIAL SUCCESS AND FREEDOM

To obtain true financial success, will depend on the motive in ones heart. With the success you will need financial freedom, for it is possible to have a lot of money, but be in financial bondage. The Holy Bible has given us many wonderful instructions, principles, policies, procedures and guidelines for us to follow, in obtaining prosperity, in all areas of our life. It is not the Will of God that we should be in debt or bondage, so it is reasonable to believe He would show us how to be free of debt. **Romans 13:8 "Let no debt remain outstanding."** It is not God's will that His children be living in poverty or suffering from the affliction of destitution.

First of all, let me say, money itself, is not evil. Yes it's true, one can, certainly have the wrong, even evil motives or desires for money, but if you do, don't expect God to bless your endeavors. Rebellion against God and His Word, will not bring His blessings about, but you could reap disaster. **1Timothy 6:10 For the love of money is at the root of all kinds of evil. And some people, craving money, have wandered from the faith and pierced themselves with many sorrows."** The Lord wants us in a position to bless others and to enjoy our life on earth. We are not to be bound up in debt, as this would prohibit us from blessing others financially, and to keep us from enjoying the life He intended for us.

Satan, of course, will work endlessly to get us in debt bondage and keep us there. He commonly uses temptation for material things, of what we want, and leads us into believing we just can't live without it. He will try to convince us, we must have it now, "because I can save so much money if I buy it now". He will use a sense of urgency so that we will buy without praying. He welcomes the use of credit cards, so we won't give much thought to what we are doing, by giving us an avenue to buy more than we intended. He is knowledgeable of the human mind set, using credit cards, of paying later and counting on, the mind will forget how much we spent and how often the card was used. On the other hand, if we use cash for our transaction, we are much more aware of how much money is going out. Vegas and the like, use chips for the same reason credit card companies want us to use their card, we will not be aware of monies spent, therefore, we will likely overspend. Satan knows how to make people feel good when they buy things, knowing this will aide in addictive behavior. When was the last time you fell into Satan's traps of temptation? **Proverbs 21:17** "**Those who love pleasure become poor; wine and luxury are not the way to riches.**"

God has given us a pathway to financial freedom and success. Giving that comes from the heart, is a place of blessings and it is a biblical principle. **Proverbs 11:25** "**A generous man will prosper**" **Luke 6:38** "**Give and it shall be given to you. A good measure, pressed down, shaken together and running over, will be poured into your lap! For with the measure you use, it will be measured to you.**" In other words, give stingy and little will be given to you. It is essential for us to develop a giving and caring heart, as this is the key to open our locked financial door. God wants to bless you so that you will be a blessing to others. This is His heart and it needs to be ours. Think of, and love others first, which will bring you blessings, but it must come from your heart, not because you want something. God loves a cheerful giver! **2 Corinthians 9:6-7** "**Remember this: Whoever sows sparingly will also reap sparingly, and whoever sows generously will also reap generously. Each man should give what he has decided in his heart to give, not reluctantly or under compulsion, for God loves a cheerful giver.**" Reap what you sow, applies to all aspects of our life. Need money, give money. Need love, give love. Need a friend, be a friend. Need support, give support. Need time, give time. This list goes on and on, but I think you get the idea.

This too, is a biblical principle "you reap what you sow." and it does work because that's how God planned it. **Proverbs 28:27 Whoever gives to the poor will lack nothing. But a curse will come upon those who close their eyes to poverty."**

God's plan for financial success is hard work. If you don't work you don't eat, and that's how it should be. **2Thessalonians 3:10 command: "Those unwilling to work will not get to eat." Proverbs 13:4,11 "Lazy people want much but get little, while the diligent are prospering". "Wealth from gambling quickly disappears; wealth from hard work grows".** Sadly as it is, too many people, today, seem to have a sense of entitlement. "you work, I eat" I am not sure how we got so far down this wrong road of *me, me, and me,* but its a very slippery slope and there will be a payback day, to come. This entitlement and selfish behavior does not bring glory to God; for this is not how He taught us to live. It is, however, the way of Satan. Once again, it comes back to, whom do we serve.

We have an inborn instinct and strong desire to be innovative and to work. We have natural predominant tendency for labor, accomplishments, creativity, to invent, or provide, and we want to be productive. It's not in our DNA to live in a nothingness state or lack of motivation. Our survival instinct is, our strongest motivation, we have to work. Don't allow an this evil world, to destroy your instincts and motivations. **Proverbs 14:23 "All hard work brings profit but mere talk leads only to poverty". Ecclesiastes 3:13 And people should eat and drink and enjoy the fruits of their labor, for these are gifts from God.**

The Lord wants us to have a day of total rest from work so we may become refreshed and rejuvenated. The body and mind both need this time to reestablish our mind sets, make adjustments and restore our vigor of youth. Most important, the seventh day of the week is, not only our day of rest, but it is the Holy Sabbath. **Leviticus 19:30 "Keep My Sabbath days of rest and show reverence toward My sanctuary, for I am the Lord". Isaiah 58:13 "Keep the Sabbath day holy. Don't pursue your own interest on that day, but enjoy the Sabbath and speak of it with delight as the Lord's holy day. Honor the Lord in everything you do.** This is the most important day of your week; and when you honor God with reverence and respect on this Holy Day; God will honor you on your work days. **Exodus 20:9 Six days a week are set apart for your daily duties and regular work.**

A fundamental principle for financial success is tithing. **Deuteronomy 14:22-23 You must set aside a tithe of your crops (income) one tenth. (23) The purpose of tithing is to teach you always to fear the LORD your God.** God is very clear and direct regarding tithing obligations. When we don't tithe, God calls this *robbing or cheating,* Him. The language of robbing or cheating God, is so powerful and convicting! The thing is, everything we have, including our own life, really belongs to God. So, when we cheat or rob God, there is a curse attached to that action. **Malachi 3:8 God says: "Should people cheat God? Yet you have cheated Me!" "You cheated Me of the tithes and offerings due to Me"** for cheating God **"you are under a curse"**!

However, there are blessings for obeying God and being honest with our tithing. Ten cents for every dollar is certainly not asking too much, considering it's all God's, anyway. God's promise for our obedience is found in **Malachi 3:10 "Bring all the tithes into the storehouse so there will be enough food in My Temple. If you do, "says the LORD Almighty, "I will open the windows of heaven for you. I will pour out a blessing so great you won't have enough room to take it in! Try it! Let Me prove it to you!"**

God's requirements apply to our personal and business life. God requires us to tithe, He commands us to be honest and ethical in all our endeavors. Our character must adhere to the highest standard of moral integrity.

Some experts seem to have a difference of opinion to whether one should tithe on their income before taxes or after taxes. Abraham gave a tenth of everything, there were no taxes. In the book of Mark, the Pharisees asked Jesus is it right to pay taxes? Jesus said in **Mark 12: 15-17 Show me a Roman coin, and I'll tell you. Whose picture and title are stamped on it? "Caesar's," they replied. Jesus said, "give to Caesar what belongs to him. But everything that belongs to God must be given to God."** The question remains, do you pay God His 10% before taxes or do you pay Him after taxes. If you are one to get a tax refund, you would, also, tithe 10% of the refund. When I get paid, IRS has already captured their take, so I pay tithing on monies actually received. I then tithe to God first, *first fruits*, then savings, bills, offerings, charity or anything else. I would suggest each person ask God and He will direct you. Because, honestly, I have been told both ways from those in the "know". What is important is our heart and obedience.

Success takes wisdom and wisdom comes from the Lord. **Proverbs 2:6 "For the Lord gives wisdom and from His mouth come knowledge and understanding. He protects the way of His faithful ones."** Whatever your vocation, career, business, or job, always keep God first and follow His direction and stay on the path He has carved out for you. **Proverbs 20:24 "A man's steps are directed by the Lord."** This, of course, is your avenue to true success. If you are just starting out with a career or business, or if you have been at your current employer for awhile and want a change, the avenue to success is all the same; do what God has planned for you and put Him first in all of your dealings!

How do you know what business or work God has planned for you; simple, just ask Him and wait for His answer. In the Bible the book of James says "you have not because you ask not". God is not limited with His communication to us, so don't put Him in a box; pray big, think big, and ask big! If you have a desire in your heart for a particular career, and that desire just won't go away, explore the possibility it is from the Lord and He his directing you. Ask Him if your desire in your heart is from Him, and, if so, ask that He open the doors; if not, ask that He close all doors that lead you in a direction that is not of Him.

Don't sabotage your opportunity for success by thinking of yourself to be all wise and you don't need God's help, for this will lead to certain failure. Yes there are many, very rich financially, people who do not believe in God, nor do they believe they need His help, because they believe their money is the only god they want or need. These are the kinds of people Jesus was talking about when He said: **Matthew 19: 23-24 "I tell you the truth, it is very hard for a rich person to get into the kingdom of Heaven. I say it is easier for a camel to go through the eye of a needle than for a rich person to enter the kingdom of God!"** These are the people that rely on their money to meet their needs, instead of God. However, without God their soul dies and whatever happiness obtained on earth is all that they will ever have, for they will be left out of the kingdom of God.

Be sure that all your riches, prosperity, and success are from God, as true success comes from the Lord, and when He blesses us with financial riches, He expect us to be a blessing to others. It is not likely that God will bless anyone financially, without first having them spiritually rich, and their heart right with Him. For success, in every area of our lives, we would need to pray for and receive wisdom, discernment, and knowledge. King Solomon prayed for wisdom and knowledge to rule properly, and God said in **2 Chronicles 1:12** **"I will certainly give you the wisdom and knowledge you requested. And I will also give you riches, wealth, and honor such as no other king has ever had before."** God is the same yesterday, today and tomorrow, for God never changes. God honors those who love, honor, trust, and obey Him. **Proverbs 2:6 "For the Lord gives wisdom! From His mouth come knowledge and understanding. He protects the way of His faithful ones." Proverbs 24:3-5 "By wisdom a house is built, and through understanding is established; through knowledge its rooms are filled with rare and beautiful treasures. A wise man has great power, a man of knowledge increases strength."**

The lord warns us to use wisdom and count the cost of our endeavors before we make our decision. A lot of people have ended up in bankruptcy court because they failed to count the cost. When we follow the Lord's basic rules we will find ourselves in the land of plenty. Not only will we be successful financially, but we will have the freedom to be a blessing to so many others as well as being successful in all areas of our own lives. We must always ask God who He wants us to bless, and wait for His answer.

Be careful with your wants. From infancy through adulthood we have an unquenchable appetite for wanting more. If we don't learn to be content with little, we will never be content with much. Keep your life free from the love of money and be content with all of God's blessings. **Hebrews 13:5 God said "Never will I leave you; never will I forsake you."** This promise is, truly, one of our richest blessings! Something worth remembering is; God said: in **Isaiah 66:2-4 "My hands have made both Heaven and earth, and they are Mine. I, the LORD, have spoken!" "I will bless those who have humble and contrite hearts, who tremble at My Word. But those who choose their own ways, delighting in their sins, are cursed. Their offerings will not be accepted." "I will send great troubles against them . . . all the things they feared."**

Let God's principles lead your motivations, instead of self greed. The Devil is always ready to create confusion, so remember the devil is into self-worship and he will go after God's moral law by encouraging us into questioning God's truth. Confusion and doubt is his strategy for our failure! Don't fall into sin by rejecting God's law, as we know, Satan will lead you into believing that you are the exception to the rule.

Do not give the Devil any part of yourself, for you are a child of God, and you were created for greatness! **1Corinthians 7:7 "Each person has a special gift from God, of one kind or another".** Don't listen, follow or believe the devil, or you will limit your potential and never achieve the greatness God put within you.

Make God the CEO of your life and business. God's successful ones put God first, family second, business-work third and then godly entertainment. Listen to God, He will direct your path right into success. Enjoy the abundant life that God has so designed for you. *Jesus came (John 10:10) so we might have an abundant life.* You were made for success, don't let it be stolen, right out from under your nose. **Psalm 112:5 Good will come to him who is generous and lends freely, who conducts his affairs with justice.**

CHAPTER SIXTEEN

Matthew 24:6-8 "You will hear of wars and rumors of wars—Such things must happen, but the end is still to come. Nation will rise against nation—there will be famines and earthquakes in various places. All these are the beginning of birth pains."

TIME IS RUNNING OUT

Everything on this earth has a beginning and an end, including earth itself. In the book of Genesis we can read about the beginning. **Genesis 1:1 "In the beginning God created the earth."** In the Book of Revelation and other books, we can read about the earth's end. **Revelation 21:1 "for the first heaven and the first earth has passed away". Ecclesiastes 3:1-2 "There is a time for everything and a reason for every activity under heaven; A time to be born and a time to die."**

Since the creation of man, in the Garden of Eden, and when sin entered the Garden, the clock started ticking toward the end of time. Absolutely. no one knows the day or hour of earth's final curtain call. **Matthew 24:36—42 "No one knows that day or hour, not even angels in heaven nor the Son, but only the Father." "Therefore, keep watch because you do not know on what day your Lord will come."**

Throughout the ages of time, we've had many self-proclaimed "prophets", giving false predictions to the day and time of Christ's return and we still have them to this very day. Their false predictions, in no way negates or nullifies the true fact that God does have us on a timetable marking the end of time. **Matthew 24:11 "and many false prophets will appear and deceive many people."** What we do know, for sure is that there is an end time coming to this earth and all life will cease to exist, whether we like it or not; but, there will be a new heaven and a new earth. What will, **not** change is God, for He will always remain the same and He will always be, the one and only, God Jehovah. **Revelation 1:8** **"I am the ALPHA (the first-the beginning) and the OMEGA (last-end) says the Lord God, who IS and who WAS, and who IS TO COME, the Almighty."**

Of course, there are many anti Christ and anti God, folks who believe this wonderful intricate human life exists because of some sort of cosmic accident or because of some type of evolution that human life was formed from other existing species or plants. These absurd theories are ridiculous, and to believe them one would have had to evolved from a plant or lower life! Fortunately, God does not need anyone's endorsement or sanctions for His truth to come to fruition. It doesn't matter if you believe God's Word or not, for what you believe has no bearing on God's truth or reality, and what *will* come to pass.

For those who do believe God's Word and accepts Jesus Christ as the only Son of God, who lived and died on the cross and was raised on the third day and is now seated at the right hand of God, will not fear the end times. Christians embrace our Lord's return with much anticipation, and know one of the benefits of accepting and following our Lord and Savior, is that He reveals His truth to His believers. We not only have the privilege of reading His Holy Scriptures, but we also are blessed to receive the Holy Spirit's clarification and understanding that allows us to hear God when He speaks to our spiritual ears and heart. The Holy Spirit is our Counselor, and is the source of all truth, and He is active in the lives of all believers. **Isaiah 11:2** **"The Spirit of the Lord will rest on him—the Spirit of Wisdom and of understanding-the Spirit of counsel and of power-the Spirit of knowledge and of fear of the Lord."** The Holy Spirit is a great gift to us from our God Jehovah! The Holy Spirit prepares our hearts and minds for the end times. This wonderful Counselor keeps us safe from the anxiety and fear that the unbelieving world must endure as we move closer to the end of God's timetable.

Although we do not know the day or hour of Jesus' return, the Lord does, tell us we will know the season and signs of the coming end. We must pay attention to His warnings and not bury our heads in the sand. The disciples asked Jesus **Matthew 24:3-6** **"What events will signal your return, and the end of the world?"**

Jesus said: "When you hear of wars and rumors of wars this does not signal my return, these must come, but the end is not yet. The nations and kingdoms of the earth will rise up against each other and there will be famines and earthquakes in many places. But all this will be only the beginning of the horrors to come." Jesus goes on to say that Christians will be hated all over the world because they belong to Him, and many Christians, **Matthew 24:10-14** "will fall back into sin and betray and hate each other". There will be many "false prophets". "Sin will be rampant everywhere and will cool the love of many." The Good News about the kingdom will be preached throughout the whole world, so that all nations will hear it, and then finally, the end will come." **Matthew 24:33-34** "When you see all these beginning to happen, you know that My return is near, even at the doors. Then at last this age will come to its close." (Jesus goes on to say) **"the world will be at ease having banquets, parties and weddings, just as it was in Noah's day before the flood".** In the book of Mark, Jesus gives us more warnings of the end to come and in the book of Luke He reiterates His warnings and adds **Luke 21:11** "There will be great earthquakes, and there will be famines and epidemics in many lands, and there will be terrifying things and great miraculous signs in the heavens." **Matthew 24:42** "So be prepared, for you don't know what day your Lord is coming."

In Noah's time there was much evil and violence and God saw and was sorry He created man. **Genesis 6:5-13** "The Lord saw how great man's wickedness on the earth had become, and that every inclination of the thoughts of mans heart was only evil all the time. The Lord grieved that He had made man on the earth, and His heart was filled with pain. So the Lord said, "I will wipe mankind, whom I have created, from the face of the earth." The earth was corrupt in God's sight and was full of violence. God said "I am going to put an end to all people and the earth."** Noah, however, found favor with God due to his righteousness. Noah was righteous and blameless among the people of his time, also, Noah walked with God and he obeyed God, so when God gave Noah instructions on how to build an Ark, Noah obeyed, even though all the people were mocking him. They didn't believe there would be a flood nor did they believe all life, outside of the Ark, would be destroyed. God kept His word, the rains came and covered the earth with water and all life outside of the Ark was destroyed.

It is a mystery to me why people, of today, do not believe God. He will repeat history and destroy this earth, and for the same reasons He did in Noah's day. Our world is as evil, if not worse, then it was in Noah's day. In this current day, as it was in Noah's time, we have parents killing their children and children killing their parents. We have fathers raping their daughters and sons, we have men and women having sexual intercourse with animals, we have homosexual acts, all of these acts, the Lord considers to be an abomination, **Leviticus 20:10-16.** Now add in murder, robbery, divorce, adultery, steeling, and abortions, just to name a very few atrocities occurring daily and that's to say nothing of all the lying, drunkenness and shameful acts of the blasphemers and what they have done to our God Jehovah. Does one really believe none of this bothers the Lord and He is just going to turn the other way? Think again, He promised to destroy all the people in Noah's day that turned from Him and He promises much worse for the end times. Yes, people today mock God and His Word just as they did in Noah's day, and the outcome will be the same.

When the Lord returns to earth to collect His followers, known as the *rapture*, it will happen quickly with no time to repent, no time to accept Jesus Christ as ones Lord and no time for even a thought, to run through your head. **1Corinthians 15:52-54 "It will happen in a moment, in the twinkling of an eye, at the last trump: For when the trumpet sounds, the Christians who have died will be raised with transformed bodies. And then we who are living will be transformed so that we will never die. When this happens-when our perishable earthly bodies have been transformed into heavenly bodies that will never die-then at last the Scriptures will come true: "Death is swallowed up in victory."**

This promise is the reason Christians are hopeful and excited for Christ's return. Christians won't be going through the horrors of the tribulation. **Matthew 24:8 "This will be the beginning of the horrors to come."** Only those left behind will endure unthinkable horror. Even the Holy Spirit will be gone from earth, at the time of the rapture. As evil as humans have become, its unimaginable what life will be like for those left behind, with no one having the Holy Spirit in them to convict or guide them from wrong doing. Think of a very, very young child that does not yet know right from wrong; they just take what they want and if you have what he wants, he will just take it away from you; because he has not, yet, been taught right from wrong. Now imagine these children are now adults and they still don't know or care about right from wrong, its all about what they want. You see, without the Holy Spirit there will be no sense of guilt, nothing in place to check what is right and what is wrong. All knowledge of right and wrong comes from God. Even though much of these moral codes have been manipulated and twisted, just think what its going to be like when all right and wrong has been eliminated from earth, along with all sense of justice. Life, at that time, will be too frightening to live, so its fortunate that God will only allow life to continue for a few short years, 3½ and then He will destroy all life.

Right now, It is not too late for you to get to know our God of Abraham, Isaac and Jacob. He is the Great I am, our God Jehovah. It's not too late to surrender your will and life over to Jesus Christ so He will be your Lord and Savior, too. Now is the time as tomorrow may be too late, for we have no promise of tomorrow. Allow God Jehovah, to be your God, today. It is not the Will of God that anyone should be left behind to perish, that is only the will of the enemy, Satan.

God wants you to prosper and live in good health. You don't need to live with a dream life in your heart, with God you can live the dream-life in reality as long as He is your First Love, your business partner, your Counselor, your Master, and your Everything. God wants you to be free, not to be bound up with the enemy's chains. God's freedom is not for you to do what you want, but it is to have the freedom to do what God has planned for you; to have your will in line with His Will, and this will bring God's favor and blessings to your precious life. God loves you more than human words can express, that's why He sacrificed His only Son on the cross, so we could have a pathway back to Him. To have the knowledge that God controls our, every breath we take, and He controls death, and He is a just, righteous and faithful without prejudice, God, and He does not change, brings the believer, much peace and comfort. **Deuteronomy 32:39** "**I Myself am He! There is no God but Me. I bring death and I give life; I wound and I heal. No one can rescue anyone from My hand.**"

There are many false gods in our world, but there is only one true God. God Jehovah, the God of Abraham, Isaac, and Jacob, the God of creation and of heaven and earth and mankind; He is the Great

"I AM". So don't allow, yourself, to be mislead with Satan's false teachings, search the Holy Bible and learn the truth for yourself. Don't blindly believe and accept what you read, hear or see as truth. Always, always check the information against God's Word. **1John 4:1-3 "Beloved, don't believe every spirit, but test the spirits, whether they are of God, because many false prophets have gone out into the world. By this you know the Spirit of God: every spirit who confesses that Yeshua (Jesus) the Messiah (Christ) has come in the flesh is of God, and every spirit who doesn't confess that Yeshua the Messiah has come in the flesh is not of God, and this is the spirit of the anti-messiah."** *TIME IS RUNNING OUT!* As for you, right now, there is still hope. Ask God to open your eyes and heart to His truth and receive our Lord and Savior, Jesus Christ, as your Lord and Savior.

ABOUT THE AUTHOR:

Bobbi Hodges, the mother of three grown, godly children and the grandmother of six children.

She has made her home in Beaverton Oregon, for the past forty five years. After thirty years in the medical field, she retired, in 2009, to devote her time to writing, fulltime.

Bobbi became a Christian fifty nine years ago, but began serious bible study twenty years ago.

To study, read and enjoy the bible, is not only a blessing, it is a wonderful privilege. Bobbi has been blessed with many study trips to Israel and has a deep love and respect for God's Holy city, Jerusalem.

Bobbi has one burning passion, and that is to help people find their way back to their creator, God Jehovah, and learn to love God and accept His many love blessings along the way. God will bless you so you can be a blessing to others.